SECOND EDITION

Oracle PL/SQL Language
Pocket Reference

Steven Feuerstein, Bill Pribyl, and Chip Dawes

Beijing · Cambridge · Farnham · Köln · Paris · Sebastopol · Taipei · Tokyo

Oracle PL/SQL Language Pocket Reference, Second Edition

by Steven Feuerstein, Bill Pribyl, and Chip Dawes

Copyright © 2003, 1999 O'Reilly & Associates, Inc. All rights reserved.
Printed in the United States of America.

Published by O'Reilly & Associates, Inc., 1005 Gravenstein Highway North, Sebastopol, CA 95472.

O'Reilly & Associates books may be purchased for educational, business, or sales promotional use. Online editions are also available for most titles (*safari.oreilly.com*). For more information, contact our corporate/institutional sales department: (800) 998-9938 or *corporate@oreilly.com*.

Editors:	Deborah Russell and Gigi Estabrook
Production Editor:	Jane Ellin
Cover Designers:	Ellie Volckhausen and Edie Freedman
Interior Designer:	Bret Kerr

Printing History:

April 1999:	First Edition.
February 2003:	Second Edition.

Nutshell Handbook, the Nutshell Handbook logo, and the O'Reilly logo are registered trademarks of O'Reilly & Associates, Inc. Many of the designations used by manufacturers and sellers to distinguish their products are claimed as trademarks. Where those designations appear in this book, and O'Reilly & Associates, Inc. was aware of a trademark claim, the designations have been printed in caps or initial caps. Oracle® and all Oracle-based trademarks and logos are trademarks or registered trademarks of Oracle Corporation, Inc. in the United States and other countries. O'Reilly & Associates, Inc. is independent of Oracle Corporation. Java and all Java-based trademarks and logos are trademarks or registered trademarks of Sun Microsystems, Inc. in the United States and other countries. O'Reilly & Associates, Inc. is independent of Sun Microsystems, Inc. The association between the image of ants and the topic of Oracle PL/SQL is a trademark of O'Reilly & Associates, Inc.

While every precaution has been taken in the preparation of this book, the publisher and authors assume no responsibility for errors or omissions, or for damages resulting from the use of the information contained herein.

0-596-00472-9
[C]   [5/03*]

Contents

Introduction	1
PL/SQL Language Fundamentals	2
PL/SQL Character Set	2
Identifiers	3
Boolean, Numeric, and String Literals	3
Datetime Interval Literals (Oracle9i)	4
Delimiters	5
Comments	6
Pragmas	7
Statements	7
Block Structure	8
Variables and Program Data	9
Scalar Datatypes	10
NLS Character Datatypes	15
LOB Datatypes	15
Implicit Datatype Conversions	16
NULLs in PL/SQL	16
Declaring Variables	16
Anchored Declarations	19
Programmer-Defined Subtypes	20

Conditional and Sequential Control — 20
- Conditional Control Statements — 20
- Sequential Control Statements — 24

Loops — 25
- Simple Loop — 26
- Numeric FOR Loop — 26
- Cursor FOR Loop — 27
- WHILE Loop — 27
- REPEAT UNTIL Loop Emulation — 28
- EXIT Statement — 28
- Loop Labels — 28

Database Interaction — 29
- Transaction Management — 29
- Autonomous Transactions — 32

Cursors in PL/SQL — 33
- Explicit Cursors — 33
- Implicit Cursors — 37
- Dynamic Cursors — 40
- Cursor Variables — 41
- Cursor Expressions — 43

Exception Handling — 44
- Declaring Exceptions — 44
- Raising Exceptions — 46
- Scope — 47
- Propagation — 47

Records in PL/SQL — 50
- Declaring Records — 50
- Referencing Fields of Records — 51
- Record Assignment — 52
- Nested Records — 53

Named Program Units — 53
- Procedures — 54
- Functions — 54
- Parameters — 56

Triggers — 65
- Creating Triggers — 65
- Trigger Predicates — 68
- DML Events — 68
- DDL Events — 69
- Database Events — 69

Packages — 69
- Package Structure — 70
- Referencing Package Elements — 72
- Package Data — 72
- SERIALLY_REUSABLE Pragma — 73
- Package Initialization — 73

Calling PL/SQL Functions in SQL — 74
- Calling a Function — 75
- Requirements and Restrictions — 76
- Calling Packaged Functions in SQL — 76
- Column/Function Name Precedence — 77

Oracle's Object-Oriented Features — 77
- Object Types — 78
- Type Inheritance (Oracle9i) — 80
- Methods — 80
- Methods in Subtypes (Oracle9i) — 83
- Manipulating Objects in PL/SQL and SQL — 84
- Upcasting and Downcasting (Oracle9i) — 85
- Changing Object Types — 88

Collections — 90
- Declaring a Collection — 91
- Initializing Collections — 92
- Adding and Removing Elements — 94
- Collection Pseudo-Functions — 94
- Collection Methods — 95
- Collections and Privileges — 98
- Nested Collections (Oracle9i) — 98
- Bulk Binds — 98

External Procedures — 102
- Creating an External Procedure — 102
- Parameters — 107

Java Language Integration — 111
- Example — 113
- Publishing Java to PL/SQL — 114
- Data Dictionary — 115

Reserved Words — 115

Index — 117

Oracle PL/SQL Language Pocket Reference

Introduction

The *Oracle PL/SQL Language Pocket Reference* is a quick reference guide to the PL/SQL programming language, which provides procedural extensions to the SQL relational database language and a range of Oracle development tools. Where a package, program, or function is supported only for a particular version of Oracle (e.g., Oracle9*i*), we indicate this in the text.

The purpose of this pocket reference is to help PL/SQL users find the syntax of specific language elements. It is not a self-contained user guide; basic knowledge of the PL/SQL programming language is required. For more information, see the following O'Reilly books:

Oracle PL/SQL Programming, Third Edition, by Steven Feuerstein with Bill Pribyl

Learning Oracle PL/SQL, by Bill Pribyl with Steven Feuerstein

Oracle Built-in Packages, by Steven Feuerstein, Charles Dye, and John Beresniewicz

Oracle PL/SQL Built-ins Pocket Reference, by Steven Feuerstein, John Beresniewicz, and Chip Dawes

Acknowledgments

Many thanks to all those who helped in the preparation of this book. In particular, thanks to first edition reviewers Eric J. Givler and Stephen Nelson and second edition reviewer Jonathan Gennick. In addition, we appreciate all the good work by the O'Reilly crew in editing and producing this book.

Conventions

UPPERCASE indicates PL/SQL keywords.

lowercase indicates user-defined items such as parameters.

Italic indicates filenames and parameters within text.

Constant width is used for code examples and output.

[ ] enclose optional items in syntax descriptions.

{ } enclose a list of items in syntax descriptions; you must choose one item from the list.

| separates bracketed list items in syntax descriptions.

PL/SQL Language Fundamentals

This section summarizes the fundamental components of the PL/SQL language: characters, identifiers, literals, delimiters, use of comments and pragmas, and construction of statements and blocks.

PL/SQL Character Set

The PL/SQL language is constructed from letters, digits, symbols, and whitespace, as defined in the following table:

Type	Characters
Letters	A-Z, a-z
Digits	0-9

Type	Characters
Symbols	`~!@#$%^&*()_-+=|[ ]{ }:;"'< >,.?/ ^`
Whitespace	`space, tab, newline, carriage return`

Characters are grouped together into four lexical units: identifiers, literals, delimiters, and comments.

Identifiers

Identifiers are names for PL/SQL objects such as constants, variables, exceptions, procedures, cursors, and reserved words. Identifiers have the following characteristics:

- Can be up to 30 characters in length
- Cannot include whitespace (space, tab, carriage return)
- Must start with a letter
- Can include a dollar sign ($), an underscore (_), and a pound sign (#)
- Are not case-sensitive

In addition, you must not use PL/SQL's reserved words as identifiers. For a list of those words, see the table in the final section in this book, "Reserved Words."

If you enclose an identifier within double quotes, then all but the first of these rules are ignored. For example, the following declaration is valid:

```
DECLARE
   "1 ^abc"  VARCHAR2(100);
BEGIN
   IF "1 ^abc" IS NULL THEN ...
END;
```

Boolean, Numeric, and String Literals

Literals are specific values not represented by identifiers. For example, TRUE, 3.14159, 6.63E-34, 'Moby Dick', and NULL are all literals of type Boolean, number, or string.

PL/SQL Language Fundamentals | 3

There are no complex datatype literals as they are internal representations. Unlike the rest of PL/SQL, literals are case-sensitive. To embed single quotes within a string literal, place two single quotes next to each other. See the following table for examples:

Literal	Actual value
'That''s Entertainment!'	That's Entertainment!
'"The Raven"'	"The Raven"
'TZ=''CDT6CST'''	TZ='CDT6CST'
''''	'
'''hello world'''	'hello world'
''''''	''

Datetime Interval Literals (Oracle9i)

The datetime interval datatypes are new with Oracle9*i*. These datatypes represent a chronological interval expressed in terms of either years and months or days, hours, minutes, seconds, and fractional seconds. Literals of these datatypes require the keyword INTERVAL followed by the literal and format string(s). The interval must go from a larger field to a smaller one, so YEAR TO MONTH is valid, but MONTH TO YEAR is not. See the following table for examples:

Literal	Actual value
INTERVAL '1-3' YEAR TO MONTH	1 year and 3 months later
INTERVAL '125-11' YEAR(3) TO MONTH	125 years and 11 months later
INTERVAL '-18' MONTH	18 months earlier
INTERVAL '-48' HOUR	48 hours earlier
INTERVAL '7 23:15' DAY TO MINUTE	7 days, 23 hours, 15 minutes later
INTERVAL '1 12:30:10.2' DAY TO SECOND	1 day, 12 hours, 30 minutes, 10.2 seconds later
INTERVAL '12:30:10.2' HOUR TO SECOND	12 hours, 30 minutes, 10.2 seconds later

Delimiters

Delimiters are symbols with special meaning, such as := (assignment operator), || (concatenation operator), and ; (statement delimiter). The following table lists the PL/SQL delimiters:

Delimiter	Description
;	Terminator (for statements and declarations)
+	Addition operator
-	Subtraction operator
*	Multiplication operator
/	Division operator
**	Exponentiation operator
||	Concatenation operator
:=	Assignment operator
=	Equality operator
<> and !=	Inequality operators
^= and ~=	Inequality operators
<	"Less than" operator
<=	"Less than or equal to" operator
>	"Greater than" operator
>=	"Greater than or equal to" operator
(and)	Expression or list delimiters
<< and >>	Label delimiters
,	(Comma) Item separator
'	(Single quote) Literal delimiter
"	(Double quote) Quoted literal delimiter
:	Host variable indicator
%	Attribute indicator
.	(Period) Component indicator (as in *record.field* or *package.element*)
@	Remote database indicator (database link)

Delimiter	Description
=>	Association operator (named notation)
..	(Two periods) Range operator (used in the FOR loop)
--	Single-line comment indicator
/* and */	Multiline comment delimiters

Comments

Comments are sections of the code that exist to aid readability. The compiler ignores them.

A single-line comment begins with a double hyphen (--) and ends with a new line. The compiler ignores all characters between the -- and the new line.

A multiline comment begins with slash asterisk (/*) and ends with asterisk slash (*/). The /* */ comment delimiters can also be used for a single-line comment. The following block demonstrates both kinds of comments:

```
DECLARE
    -- Two dashes comment out only the physical line.
    /* Everything is a comment until the compiler
       encounters the following symbol */
```

You cannot embed multiline comments within a multiline comment, so be careful during development if you comment out portions of code that include comments. The following code demonstrates this issue:

```
DECLARE
    /* Everything is a comment until the compiler
       /* This comment inside another WON'T work!*/
       encounters the following symbol. */

    /* Everything is a comment until the compiler
       -- This comment inside another WILL work!
       encounters the following symbol. */
```

Pragmas

The PRAGMA keyword is used to give instructions to the compiler. There are four types of pragmas in PL/SQL:

EXCEPTION_INIT
    Tells the compiler to associate the specified error number with an identifier that has been declared an EXCEPTION in your current program or an accessible package. See the "Exception Handling" section for more information on this pragma.

RESTRICT_REFERENCES
    Tells the compiler the purity level of a packaged program. The purity level is the degree to which a program does not read/write database tables and/or package variables. See the "Calling PL/SQL Functions in SQL" section for more information on this pragma.

SERIALLY_REUSABLE
    Tells the runtime engine that package data should not persist between references. This is used to reduce per-user memory requirements when the package data is only needed for the duration of the call and not for the duration of the session. See the "Packages" section for more information on this pragma.

AUTONOMOUS_TRANSACTION
    Starting in Oracle8*i*, tells the compiler that the function, procedure, top-level anonymous PL/SQL block, object method, or database trigger executes in its own transaction space. See the "Database Interaction" section for more information on this pragma.

Statements

A PL/SQL program is composed of one or more logical statements. A *statement* is terminated by a semicolon delimiter. The physical end-of-line marker in a PL/SQL program is ignored by the compiler, except to terminate a single-line comment (initiated by the -- symbol).

Block Structure

Each PL/SQL program is a *block* consisting of a standard set of elements, identified by keywords (see Figure 1). The block determines the scope of declared elements, and how exceptions are handled and propagated. A block can be anonymous or named. Named blocks include functions, procedures, packages, and triggers.

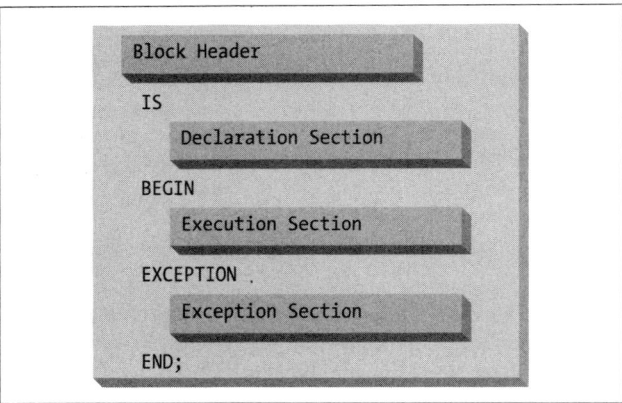

Figure 1. The PL/SQL block structure

Here is an example of an anonymous block:

```
DECLARE
   today DATE DEFAULT SYSDATE;
BEGIN
   -- Display the date.
   DBMS_OUTPUT.PUT_LINE ('Today is ' || today);
END;
```

Here is a named block that performs the same action:

```
CREATE OR REPLACE PROCEDURE show_the_date
IS
   today DATE DEFAULT SYSDATE;
BEGIN
   -- Display the date.
```

```
    DBMS_OUTPUT.PUT_LINE ('Today is ' || today);
END show_the_date;
```

The following table summarizes the sections of a PL/SQL block:

Section	Description
Header	Required for named blocks. Specifies the way the program is called by other PL/SQL blocks. Anonymous blocks do not have a header. They start with the DECLARE keyword if there is a declaration section, or with the BEGIN keyword if there are no declarations.
Declaration	Optional; declares variables, cursors, TYPEs, and local programs that are used in the block's execution and exception sections.
Execution	Optional in package and TYPE specifications; contains statements that are executed when the block is run.
Exception	Optional; describes error-handling behavior for exceptions raised in the executable section.

Variables and Program Data

PL/SQL programs are normally used to manipulate database information. You commonly do this by declaring variables and data structures in your programs, and then working with that PL/SQL-specific data.

A *variable* is a named instantiation of a data structure declared in a PL/SQL block (either locally or in a package). Unless you declare a variable as a CONSTANT, its value can be changed at any time in your program.

The following table summarizes the different types of program data:

Type	Description
Scalar	Variables made up of a single value, such as a number, date, or Boolean
Composite	Variables made up of multiple values, such as a record or a collection
Reference	Pointers to values
LOB	Variables containing large object (LOB) locators

Scalar Datatypes

Scalar datatypes divide into four families: number, character, datetime, and Boolean.

Numeric datatypes

Numeric datatypes are further divided into decimal, binary integer, and PLS_INTEGER storage types.

Decimal numeric datatypes store fixed and floating-point numbers of just about any size. They include NUMBER, DEC, DECIMAL, NUMERIC, FLOAT, REAL, and DOUBLE PRECISION. The maximum precision of a variable with type NUMBER is 38 digits, which yields a range of values from 1.0E-129 through 9.999E125. (This range of numbers would include the mass of an electron over the mass of the universe or the size of the universe in angstroms.)

Variables of type NUMBER can be declared with precision and scale, as follows:

```
NUMBER(precision, scale)
```

where *precision* is the number of digits, and *scale* is the number of digits to the right (positive scale) or left (negative scale) of the decimal point at which rounding occurs. Legal values for *scale* range from -84 to 127. The following table shows examples of *precision* and *scale*:

Declaration	Assigned value	Stored value
NUMBER	6.02	6.02
NUMBER(4)	8675	8675
NUMBER(4)	8675309	Error
NUMBER(12,5)	3.14159265	3.14159
NUMBER(12,-5)	8675309	8700000

Binary integer numeric datatypes store whole numbers. They include BINARY_INTEGER, INTEGER, INT, SMALLINT,

NATURAL, NATURALN, POSITIVE, POSITIVEN, and SIGNTYPE. Binary integer datatypes store signed integers in the range of $-2^{31} + 1$ to $2^{31} - 1$. The subtypes include NATURAL (0 through 2^{31}) and POSITIVE (1 through 2^{31}) together with the NOT NULL variations NATURALN and POSITIVEN. SIGNTYPE is restricted to three values (-1, 0, 1).

PLS_INTEGER datatypes have the same range as the BINARY_INTEGER datatype, but use machine arithmetic instead of library arithmetic, so are slightly faster for computation-heavy processing.

The following table lists the PL/SQL numeric datatypes with ANSI and IBM compatibility. In this table:

- *prec* is the precision for the subtype.
- *scale* is the scale of the subtype.
- *binary* is the binary precision of the subtype.

PL/SQL datatype	Compatibility	Oracle RDBMS datatype
DEC(*prec,scale*)	ANSI	NUMBER(*prec,scale*)
DECIMAL(*prec,scale*)	IBM	NUMBER(*prec,scale*)
DOUBLE PRECISION	ANSI	NUMBER
FLOAT(*binary*)	ANSI, IBM	NUMBER
INT	ANSI	NUMBER(38)
INTEGER	ANSI, IBM	NUMBER(38)
NUMERIC(*prec,scale*)	ANSI	NUMBER(*prec,scale*)
REAL	ANSI	NUMBER
SMALLINT	ANSI, IBM	NUMBER(38)

Character datatypes

Character datatypes store alphanumeric text and are manipulated by character functions. As with the numeric family, there are several subtypes in the character family, shown in the following table:

Family	Description
CHAR	Fixed-length alphanumeric strings. Valid sizes are 1 to 32767 bytes (which is larger than the Oracle database limit of 4000).
VARCHAR2	Variable-length alphanumeric strings. Valid sizes are 1 to 32767 bytes (which is larger than the Oracle database limit of 4000).
LONG	Variable-length alphanumeric strings. Valid sizes are 1 to 32760 bytes. LONG is included primarily for backward compatibility. CLOB is the preferred datatype for large character strings.
RAW	Variable-length binary strings. Valid sizes are 1 to 32767 bytes (which is larger than the Oracle database limit of 2000). RAW data do not undergo character set conversion when selected from a remote database.
LONG RAW	Variable-length binary strings. Valid sizes are 1 to 32760 bytes. LONG RAW is included primarily for backward compatibility. BLOB and BFILE are the preferred datatypes for large binary data.
ROWID	Fixed-length binary data. Every row in a database has a physical address or ROWID. A ROWID has four parts in base 64: *OOOOOOFFFFBBBBBBBBRRR* where: *OOOOOO* is the object number. *FFFF* is the absolute or relative file number. *BBBBBBBB* is the block number within the file. *RRRR* is the row number within the block.
UROWID	Universal ROWID. Variable-length hexadecimal string depicting a logical, physical, or non-Oracle row identifier. Valid sizes are up to 4000 bytes.

Datetime datatypes

Oracle expanded support for datetime data in Oracle9*i* by introducing an assortment of new datatypes. The datetime datatypes are DATE (the only datetime datatype pre-Oracle9*i*), TIMESTAMP, TIMESTAMP WITH TIME ZONE, and TIMESTAMP WITH LOCAL TIME ZONE. The two interval datatypes, also new to Oracle9*i*, are INTERVAL YEAR TO MONTH and INTERVAL DAY TO SECOND.

DATE values are fixed-length, date-plus-time values. The DATE datatype can store dates from January 1, 4712 B.C. to December 31, 9999 A.D. Each DATE includes the century, year, month, day, hour, minute, and second. Sub-second granularity is not supported via the DATE datatype; use one of the TIMESTAMP datatypes instead. The time portion of a DATE defaults to midnight (12:00:00 AM) if it is not included explicitly.

TIMESTAMP values store date and time to sub-second granularity. The sub-second precision (the number of digits to the right of the decimal) either defaults or is set to 0 through 9 digits by declaration, as in:

```
DECLARE
   mytime_declared TIMESTAMP(9);
   mytime_default  TIMESTAMP;
```

The default precision is 6 digits of precision to the right of the decimal.

TIMESTAMP WITH TIME ZONE values store date and time values like a TIMESTAMP but also store the hourly offset from UTC (Coordinated Universal Time, which is essentially equivalent to Greenwich Mean Time). As with TIMESTAMP, the sub-second precision is 0 to 9 digits, either declared or inherited from the default 6 digits of precision.

```
DECLARE
   mytime_declared TIMESTAMP(9) WITH TIME ZONE;
   mytime_default  TIMESTAMP WITH TIME ZONE;
```

TIMESTAMP WITH LOCAL TIME ZONE values store date and time values together with the UTC offset, like a TIMESTAMP WITH TIME ZONE. The principal difference between these timestamp datatypes occurs when values are saved to or retrieved from a database table. TIMESTAMP WITH LOCAL TIME ZONE values are converted to the database time zone and saved without an offset. The values retrieved from the database table are converted from the database time zone to the session's time zone.

The offset from UTC for both TIMESTAMP WITH TIME ZONE and TIMESTAMP WITH LOCAL TIME ZONE can be hours and minutes or a time zone region (found in the V$TIMEZONE_NAMES data dictionary view) with the optional daylight savings time name (also found in V$TIMEZONE_NAMES). For example:

```
ALTER SESSION SET NLS_TIMESTAMP_TZ_FORMAT=
   'DD-Mon-YYYY HH24:MI:SS.FF TZR';
DECLARE
   my_tswtz     TIMESTAMP(4) WITH TIME ZONE;
BEGIN
   my_tswtz := '31-JUL-02 07:32:45.1234 US/Pacific';
```

INTERVAL YEAR TO MONTH values store a period of time in years and months:

```
DECLARE
   myy2m INTERVAL YEAR TO MONTH;
BEGIN
   myy2m := INTERVAL '1-6' YEAR TO MONTH;
```

INTERVAL DAY TO SECOND values store a period of time in days, hours, minutes, seconds, and fractional seconds:

```
DECLARE
   myd2s INTERVAL DAY TO SECOND;
BEGIN
   myd2s := INTERVAL '2 10:32:15.678' DAY TO SECOND;
```

Boolean datatype

The BOOLEAN datatype can store one of only three values: TRUE, FALSE, or NULL. BOOLEAN variables are usually used in logical control structures such as IF...THEN or LOOP statements.

The following truth tables show the results of logical AND, OR, and NOT operations with PL/SQL's three-value Boolean model:

AND	TRUE	FALSE	NULL
TRUE	TRUE	FALSE	NULL
FALSE	FALSE	FALSE	FALSE
NULL	NULL	FALSE	NULL

OR	TRUE	FALSE	NULL
TRUE	TRUE	TRUE	TRUE
FALSE	TRUE	FALSE	NULL
NULL	TRUE	NULL	NULL

NOT (TRUE)	NOT (FALSE)	NOT (NULL)
FALSE	TRUE	NULL

NLS Character Datatypes

The standard WE8MSWIN1252 or WE8ISO8859P2 character set does not support some languages, such as Chinese and Greek. To support a secondary character set, Oracle allows two character sets in a database—the database character set and the national character set (NLS).

The two NLS datatypes, NCHAR and NVARCHAR2, are used to represent data in the national character set. NCHAR values are fixed-length character data; the maximum length is 32767 bytes. NVARCHAR2 values are variable-length character data; the maximum length is also 32767 bytes.

LOB Datatypes

PL/SQL supports a number of large object (LOB) datatypes, which can store objects of up to four gigabytes of data. Unlike the scalar datatypes, variables declared for LOBs use locators, or pointers to the actual data. LOBs are manipulated in PL/SQL using the built-in package DBMS_LOB. The LOB datatypes are:

BFILE
: File locators pointing to read-only large binary objects in operating system files. With BFILEs, the large objects are outside the database.

BLOB
: LOB locators that point to large binary objects inside the database.

CLOB
   LOB locators that point to large character (alphanumeric) objects inside the database.

NCLOB
   LOB locators that point to large national character set objects inside the database.

Implicit Datatype Conversions

Whenever PL/SQL detects that a datatype conversion is necessary, it attempts to change the values as required to perform the operation. Figure 2 shows what types of implicit conversions PL/SQL can perform.

NULLs in PL/SQL

PL/SQL represents unknown or inapplicable values as NULL values. Because a NULL is unknown, a NULL is never equal or not equal to anything (including another NULL value). In addition, most functions return a NULL when passed a NULL argument—the notable exceptions are NVL, NVL2, CONCAT, and REPLACE. You cannot check for equality or inequality to NULL; therefore, you must use the IS NULL or IS NOT NULL syntax to check for NULL values.

Here is an example of the IS NULL syntax used to check the value of a variable:

```
BEGIN
   IF myvar IS NULL
   THEN
      ...
```

Declaring Variables

Before you can use a variable, you must first declare it in the declaration section of your PL/SQL block or in a package as a global. When you declare a variable, PL/SQL allocates memory for the variable's value and names the storage

From \ To	BINARY_INTEGER	BLOB	CHAR	CLOB	DATE	LONG	NUMBER	PLS_INTEGER	RAW	UROWID	VARCHAR2
BINARY_INTEGER	NA		●			●	●	●			●
BLOB		NA							●		
CHAR	●		NA	●	●	●	●	●	●	●	●
CLOB			●	NA							●
DATE			●		NA	●					●
LONG			●			NA			●		●
NUMBER	●		●			●	NA	●			●
PLS_INTEGER	●		●			●	●	NA			●
RAW		●	●			●			NA		●
UROWID			●							NA	●
VARCHAR2	●		●	●	●	●	●	●	●	●	NA

Figure 2. Implicit conversions performed by PL/SQL

Variables and Program Data | 17

location so that the value can be retrieved and changed. The syntax for a variable declaration is:

```
variable_name datatype [CONSTANT] [NOT NULL]
    [{ := | DEFAULT } initial_value]
```

Constrained declarations

The datatype in a declaration can be constrained or unconstrained. Constrained datatypes have a size, scale, or precision limit that is less than the unconstrained datatype. For example:

```
total_sales    NUMBER(15,2);   -- Constrained.
emp_id         VARCHAR2(9);    -- Constrained.
company_number NUMBER;         -- Unconstrained.
book_title     VARCHAR2;       -- Not valid.
```

Constrained declarations require less memory than unconstrained declarations. Not all datatypes can be specified as unconstrained. You cannot, for example, declare a variable to be of type VARCHAR2. You must always specify the maximum size of a variable-length string.

Constants

The CONSTANT keyword in a declaration requires an initial value and does not allow that value to be changed. For example:

```
min_order_qty   NUMBER(1) CONSTANT := 5;
```

Default values

Whenever you declare a variable, it is assigned a default value of NULL. Initializing all variables is distinctive to PL/SQL; in this way, PL/SQL differs from languages such as C and Ada. If you want to initialize a variable to a value other than NULL, you do so in the declaration with either the assignment operator (:=) or the DEFAULT keyword:

```
counter   BINARY_INTEGER := 0;
priority  VARCHAR2(8)    DEFAULT 'LOW';
```

A NOT NULL constraint can be appended to the variable's datatype declaration to indicate that NULL is not a valid value. If you add the NOT NULL constraint, you must explicitly assign an initial value for that variable.

Anchored Declarations

Use the %TYPE attribute to *anchor* the datatype of a scalar variable to either another variable or to a column in a database table or view. Use %ROWTYPE to anchor a record's declaration to a cursor or table (see the "Records in PL/SQL" section for more detail on the %ROWTYPE attribute).

The following block shows several variations of anchored declarations:

```
DECLARE
   tot_sales NUMBER(20,2);
   -- Anchor to a PL/SQL variable.
   monthly_sales tot_sales%TYPE;

   -- Anchor to a database column.
   v_ename employee.last_name%TYPE;

   CURSOR mycur IS
      SELECT * FROM employee;

   -- Anchor to a cursor.
   myrec mycur%ROWTYPE;
```

The NOT NULL clause on a variable declaration (but not on a database column definition) follows the %TYPE anchoring and requires anchored declarations to have a default in their declaration. The default value for an anchored declaration can be different from that for the base declaration:

```
tot_sales      NUMBER(20,2) NOT NULL DEFAULT 0;
monthly_sales  tot_sales%TYPE DEFAULT 10;
```

Programmer-Defined Subtypes

PL/SQL allows you to define unconstrained scalar subtypes. An unconstrained subtype provides an alias to the original underlying datatype; for example:

```
CREATE OR REPLACE PACKAGE std_types
IS
   -- Declare standard types as globals.
   SUBTYPE dollar_amt_t IS NUMBER;
END std_types;

CREATE OR REPLACE PROCEDURE process_money
IS
   -- Use the global type declared above.
   credit std_types.dollar_amt_t;
   ...
```

A constrained subtype limits or constrains the new datatype to a subset of the original datatype. For example, POSITIVE is a constrained subtype of BINARY_INTEGER. The declaration for POSITIVE in the STANDARD package is:

```
SUBTYPE POSITIVE IS BINARY_INTEGER RANGE 1..2147483647;
```

You can define your own constrained subtypes in your programs:

```
PACKAGE std_types
IS
   SUBTYPE currency_t IS NUMBER (15, 2);

END;
```

Conditional and Sequential Control

PL/SQL includes conditional (IF, CASE) structures as well as sequential control (GOTO, NULL) constructs.

Conditional Control Statements

There are several varieties of IF-THEN-ELSE and CASE structures.

IF-THEN combination

```
IF condition THEN
   executable statement(s)
END IF;
```

For example:

```
IF caller_type = 'VIP' THEN
   generate_response('GOLD');
END IF;
```

IF-THEN-ELSE combination

```
IF condition THEN
   TRUE sequence_of_executable_statement(s)
ELSE
   FALSE/NULL sequence_of_executable_statement(s)
END IF;
```

For example:

```
IF caller_type = 'VIP' THEN
   generate_response('GOLD');
ELSE
   generate_response('BRONZE');
END IF;
```

IF-THEN-ELSIF combination

```
IF condition-1 THEN
   statements-1
ELSIF condition-N THEN
 statements-N
[ELSE
   ELSE statements]
END IF;
```

For example:

```
IF caller_type = 'VIP' THEN
   generate_response('GOLD');
ELSIF priority_client THEN
   generate_response('SILVER');
ELSE
   generate_response('BRONZE');
END IF;
```

Conditional and Sequential Control

CASE statement (Oracle9i)

There are two types of CASE statements: simple and searched.

A simple CASE statement is similar to an IF-THEN-ELSIF structure. The statement has a switch expression immediately after the keyword CASE. The expression is evaluated and compared to the value in each WHEN clause. The first WHEN clause with a matching value is executed and then control passes to the next statement following the END CASE. For example:

```
CASE region_id
   WHEN 'NE' THEN
      mgr_name := 'MINER';
   WHEN 'SE' THEN
      mgr_name := 'KOOI';
   ELSE mgr_name := 'LANE';
END CASE;
```

If a switch expression evaluates to NULL, the ELSE case is the only one that can possibly match; WHEN NULL will never match because Oracle performs an equality comparison on the expressions.

Both the CASE statement and the CASE expression (see the next section) should include an ELSE clause that will execute statements if no WHEN clause evaluates TRUE, because PL/SQL's runtime engine will raise an exception if it finds no matching expression.

The searched CASE statement does not have a switch; instead, each WHEN clause has a complete Boolean expression. The first matching WHEN clause is executed and control passes to the next statement following the END CASE. For example:

```
CASE
   WHEN region_id = 'EAME' THEN
      mgr_name := 'SCHMIDT';
   WHEN division = 'SALES' THEN
      mgr_name := 'KENNEDY';
```

```
      ELSE mgr_name := 'GUPTA';
END CASE;
```

CASE expression (Oracle9i)

There are also two types of CASE expressions: simple and searched. You can use CASE expressions anywhere that you can use any other type of expressions in PL/SQL programs.

A simple CASE expression lets you choose an expression to evaluate based on a scalar value that you provide as input. The following example shows a simple CASE expression being used with the built-in DBMS_OUTPUT package to output the value of a Boolean variable. DBMS.OUTPUT. PUT_LINE is not overloaded to handle Boolean types, so in this example the CASE expression converts the Boolean value in a character string, which PUT_LINE can then handle:

```
DECLARE
    boolean_true BOOLEAN := TRUE;
    boolean_false BOOLEAN := FALSE;
    boolean_null BOOLEAN;

    FUNCTION boolean_to_varchar2 (flag IN BOOLEAN)
       RETURN VARCHAR2 IS
    BEGIN
       RETURN
       CASE flag
       WHEN TRUE THEN 'True'
       WHEN FALSE THEN 'False'
       ELSE 'NULL' END;
    END;

BEGIN
    DBMS_OUTPUT.PUT_LINE(boolean_to_varchar2(boolean_true));
    DBMS_OUTPUT.PUT_LINE(boolean_to_varchar2(boolean_false));
    DBMS_OUTPUT.PUT_LINE(boolean_to_varchar2(boolean_null));
END;
```

A searched CASE expression evaluates a list of expressions to find the first one that evaluates to TRUE, and then returns the results of an associated expression. In the following example, a searched CASE expression returns the proper bonus value for any given salary:

```
DECLARE
  salary NUMBER := 20000;
  employee_id NUMBER := 36325;

  PROCEDURE give_bonus
    (emp_id IN NUMBER, bonus_amt IN NUMBER) IS
  BEGIN
    DBMS_OUTPUT.PUT_LINE(emp_id);
    DBMS_OUTPUT.PUT_LINE(bonus_amt);
  END;

BEGIN
   give_bonus(employee_id,
          CASE
          WHEN salary >= 10000 AND salary <=20000 THEN 1500
          WHEN salary > 20000 AND salary <= 40000 THEN 1000
          WHEN salary > 40000 THEN 500
          ELSE 0
          END);
END;
```

Sequential Control Statements

PL/SQL provides a GOTO statement and a NULL statement to aid in sequential control operations.

GOTO

The GOTO statement performs unconditional branching to a named label. You should only rarely use a GOTO. At least one executable statement must follow the label (the NULL statement can be this necessary executable statement). The format of a GOTO statement is:

```
GOTO <<label_name>>;
```

For example:

```
BEGIN
   GOTO second_output;

   DBMS_OUTPUT.PUT_LINE('This line will never execute.');
```

```
    <<second_output>>
    DBMS_OUPUT.PUT_LINE('We are here!');
END
```

There are a number of scope restrictions on where a GOTO can branch control. A GOTO:

- Can branch out of an IF statement, LOOP, or sub-block
- Cannot branch into an IF statement, LOOP, or sub-block
- Cannot branch from one section of an IF statement to another (from the IF-THEN section to the ELSE section is illegal)
- Cannot branch into or out of a sub-program
- Cannot branch from the exception section to the executable section of a PL/SQL block
- Cannot branch from the executable section to the exception section of a PL/SQL block, although a RAISE does this

NULL

The NULL statement is an executable statement that does nothing. It is useful when an executable statement must follow a GOTO label or to aid readability in an IF-THEN-ELSE structure. For example:

```
IF :report.selection = 'DETAIL' THEN
   exec_detail_report;
ELSE
   NULL;
END IF;
```

Loops

The LOOP construct allows you to execute a sequence of statements repeatedly. There are three kind of loops: simple (infinite), FOR, and WHILE.

You can use the EXIT statement to break out of LOOP and pass control to the statement following the END LOOP.

Simple Loop

```
LOOP
   executable_statement(s)
END LOOP;
```

The simple loop should contain an EXIT or EXIT WHEN unless you want it to execute infinitely. Use the simple loop when you want the body of the loop to execute at least once. For example:

```
LOOP
   FETCH company_cur INTO company_rec;
   EXIT WHEN company_cur%ROWCOUNT > 5 OR
      company_cur%NOTFOUND;
   process_company(company_cur);
END LOOP;
```

Numeric FOR Loop

```
FOR loop_index IN [REVERSE] lowest_number..highest_number
LOOP
   executable_statement(s)
END LOOP;
```

The PL/SQL runtime engine automatically declares the loop index a PLS_INTEGER variable; never declare a variable with that name yourself. The *lowest_number* and *highest_number* ranges can be variables, but are evaluated only once—on initial entry into the loop. The REVERSE keyword causes PL/SQL to start with the *highest_number* and decrement down to the *lowest_number*. For example, this code:

```
BEGIN
   FOR counter IN 1 .. 4
   LOOP
      DBMS_OUTPUT.PUT(counter);
   END LOOP;
   DBMS_OUTPUT.NEW_LINE;

   FOR counter IN REVERSE 1 .. 4
   LOOP
      DBMS_OUTPUT.PUT(counter);
   END LOOP;
   DBMS_OUTPUT.NEW_LINE;END;
```

yields the following output:

```
1234
4321
```

Cursor FOR Loop

```
FOR record_index IN [cursor_name | (SELECT statement)]
LOOP
   executable_statement(s)
END LOOP;
```

The PL/SQL runtime engine automatically declares the loop index a record of *cursor_name*%ROWTYPE; never declare a variable with that name yourself.

The cursor FOR loop automatically opens the cursor, fetches all rows identified by the cursor, and then closes the cursor. You can embed the SELECT statement directly in the cursor FOR loop. For example:

```
FOR emp_rec IN emp_cur
LOOP
   IF emp_rec.title = 'Oracle Programmer'
   THEN
      give_raise(emp_rec.emp_id,30)
   END IF;
END LOOP;
```

WHILE Loop

```
WHILE condition
LOOP
   executable_statement(s)
END LOOP;
```

Use the WHILE loop in cases where you may not want the loop body to execute even once:

```
WHILE NOT end_of_analysis
LOOP
   perform_analysis;
   get_next_record;
   IF analysis_cursor%NOTFOUND AND next_step IS NULL
   THEN
```

Loops | 27

```
      end_of_analysis := TRUE;
   END IF;
END LOOP;
```

REPEAT UNTIL Loop Emulation

PL/SQL does not directly support a REPEAT UNTIL construct, but a modified simple loop can emulate one. The syntax for this emulated REPEAT UNTIL loop is:

```
LOOP
   executable_statement(s)
   EXIT WHEN Boolean_condition;
END LOOP;
```

Use the emulated REPEAT UNTIL loop when executing iterations indefinitely before conditionally terminating the loop.

EXIT Statement

```
EXIT [WHEN condition];
```

If you do not include a WHEN clause in the EXIT statement, it will terminate the loop unconditionally. Otherwise, the loop terminates only if the Boolean *condition* evaluates to TRUE. The EXIT statement is optional and can appear anywhere in the loop.

Loop Labels

Loops can be optionally labeled to improve readability and execution control, as we showed earlier in the discussion of the GOTO statement. The label must appear immediately in front of the statement that initiates the loop.

The following example demonstrates the use of loop labels to qualify variables within a loop and also to terminate nested and outer loops:

```
<<year_loop>>
FOR yearind IN 1 .. 20
LOOP
   <<month_loop>>
```

```
   LOOP
      ...
      IF year_loop.yearind > 10
      THEN
         EXIT year_loop;
      END IF;
   END LOOP month_loop;
END LOOP year_loop;
```

Database Interaction

PL/SQL is tightly integrated with the underlying SQL layer of the Oracle database. You can execute SQL statements (UPDATE, INSERT, DELETE, MERGE, and SELECT) directly in PL/SQL programs. You can also execute Data Definition Language (DDL) statements through the use of dynamic SQL. In addition, you can manage transactions with COMMIT, ROLLBACK, and other Data Control Language (DCL) statements.

Transaction Management

The Oracle RDBMS provides a transaction model based on a unit of work. The PL/SQL language supports most, but not all, of the database model for transactions (you cannot, for example, specify ROLLBACK FORCE). A transaction begins with the first change to data and ends with either a COMMIT or a ROLLBACK. Transactions are independent of PL/SQL blocks. Transactions can span multiple PL/SQL blocks, or there can be multiple transactions in a single PL/SQL block. The PL/SQL-supported transaction statements include COMMIT, ROLLBACK, SAVEPOINT, SET TRANSACTION, and LOCK TABLE, described in the following sections.

COMMIT

```
COMMIT [WORK] [COMMENT text];
```

COMMIT makes the database changes permanent and visible to other database sessions. The WORK keyword is optional and only aids readability—it is rarely used. The COMMENT text is optional and can be up to 50 characters in length. It is only germane to in-doubt distributed (two-phase commit) transactions. The database statement COMMIT FORCE, also for distributed transactions, is not supported in PL/SQL.

ROLLBACK

```
ROLLBACK [WORK] [TO [SAVEPOINT] savepoint_name];
```

ROLLBACK undoes the changes made in the current transaction either to the beginning of the transaction or to a *savepoint*. A savepoint is a named processing point in a transaction, created with the SAVEPOINT statement. Rolling back to a savepoint is a partial rollback of a transaction, wiping out all changes (and savepoints) that occurred later than the named savepoint.

SAVEPOINT

```
SAVEPOINT savepoint_name;
```

SAVEPOINT establishes a savepoint in the current transaction. *savepoint_name* is an undeclared identifier—you do not declare it. More than one savepoint can be established within a transaction. If you reuse a savepoint name, that savepoint is moved to the later position and you will not be able to roll back to the initial savepoint position.

SET TRANSACTION

```
SET TRANSACTION READ ONLY;
SET TRANSACTION ISOLATION LEVEL SERIALIZABLE;
SET TRANSACTION USE ROLLBACK SEGMENT rbseg_name;
```

SET TRANSACTION has three transaction control functions:

READ ONLY
  Marks the beginning of a read-only transaction. This indicates to the RDBMS that a read-consistent view of the database is to be enforced for the transaction (the

default is for the statement). This read-consistent view means that only changes committed before the transaction begins are visible for the duration of the transaction. The transaction is ended with either a COMMIT or a ROLLBACK. Only LOCK TABLE, SELECT, SELECT INTO, OPEN, FETCH, CLOSE, COMMIT, or ROLLBACK statements are permitted during a read-only transaction. Issuing other statements, such as INSERT or UPDATE, in a read-only transaction results in an ORA-1456 error.

ISOLATION LEVEL SERIALIZABLE
Similar to a READ ONLY transaction in that transaction-level read consistency is enforced instead of the default statement-level read consistency. Serializable transactions do allow changes to data, however.

USE ROLLBACK SEGMENT
Tells the RDBMS to use the specifically named rollback segment *rbseg_name*. This statement is useful when only one rollback segment is large, and a program knows that it needs to use the large rollback segment, such as during a month-end close operation. For example, if we know that our large rollback segment is named rbs_large, we can tell the database to use it by issuing the following statement before our first change to data:

```
SET TRANSACTION USE ROLLBACK SEGMENT rbs_large;
```

LOCK TABLE

```
LOCK TABLE table_list IN lock_mode MODE [NOWAIT];
```

This statement bypasses the implicit database row-level locks by explicitly locking one or more tables in the specified mode. The *table_list* is a comma-delimited list of tables. The *lock_mode* is one of the following: ROW SHARE, ROW EXCLUSIVE, SHARE UPDATE, SHARE, SHARE ROW EXCLUSIVE, or EXCLUSIVE. The NOWAIT keyword specifies that the RDBMS should not wait for a lock to be released. If there is a lock when NOWAIT is specified, the

RDBMS raises the exception "ORA-00054: resource busy and acquire with NOWAIT specified." The default RDBMS locking behavior is to wait indefinitely.

Autonomous Transactions

Autonomous transactions, introduced in Oracle8*i*, execute within a block of code as separate transactions from the outer (main) transaction. Changes can be committed or rolled back in an autonomous transaction without committing or rolling back the main transaction. Changes committed in an autonomous transaction are visible to the main transaction, even though they occur after the start of the main transaction. Those changes committed in an autonomous transaction are visible to other transactions as well. The RDBMS suspends the main transaction while the autonomous transaction executes:

```
PROCEDURE main IS
BEGIN
   UPDATE ...  -- Main transaction begins here.
   DELETE ...
   at_proc;    -- Call the autonomous transaction.
   SELECT ...
   INSERT ...
   COMMIT;     -- Main transaction ends here.
END;

PROCEDURE at_proc IS
   PRAGMA AUTONOMOUS_TRANSACTION;
BEGIN          -- Main transaction suspends here.
   SELECT ...
   INSERT ...  -- Autonomous transaction begins here.
   UPDATE ...
   DELETE ...
   COMMIT;     -- Autonomous transaction ends here.
END;           -- Main transaction resumes here.
```

So, changes made in the main transaction are not visible to the autonomous transaction, and if the main transaction holds any locks that the autonomous transaction waits for, a deadlock occurs. Using the NOWAIT option on UPDATE statements in autonomous transactions can help to minimize this kind of deadlock. Functions and procedures (local program, standalone, or packaged), database triggers, top-level anonymous PL/SQL blocks, and object methods can be declared autonomous via the compiler directive PRAGMA AUTONOMOUS_TRANSACTION. In addition, there must be a commit or a rollback at each exit point in the autonomous program.

Cursors in PL/SQL

Every SQL statement executed by the RDBMS has a private SQL area that contains information about the SQL statement and the set of data returned. In PL/SQL, a *cursor* is a name assigned to a specific private SQL area for a specific SQL statement. There can be either static cursors, whose SQL statement is determined at compile time, or dynamic cursors, whose SQL statement is determined at runtime. Static cursors are used only for DML statements (SELECT, INSERT, UPDATE, DELETE, MERGE, or SELECT FOR UPDATE). These static cursors can be explicitly declared and named or may appear in-line as an implicit cursor. Dynamic cursors are used for any type of valid SQL statement including DDL (CREATE, TRUNCATE, ALTER) and DCL (GRANT, REVOKE). Dynamic cursors are implemented with the EXECUTE IMMEDIATE statement.

Explicit Cursors

Explicit cursors are SELECT statements that are DECLAREd explicitly in the declaration section of the current block or in a package specification. Use OPEN, FETCH, and CLOSE in the execution or exception sections of your programs.

Declaring explicit cursors

To use an explicit cursor, you must first declare it in the declaration section of a block or package. There are three types of explicit cursor declarations:

- A cursor without parameters; for example:

    ```
    CURSOR company_cur
       IS
       SELECT company_id FROM company;
    ```

- A cursor that accepts arguments through a parameter list; for example:

    ```
    CURSOR company_cur (id_in IN NUMBER) IS
    SELECT name FROM company
    WHERE  company_id = id_in;
    ```

- A cursor header that contains a RETURN clause in place of the SELECT statement; for example:

    ```
    CURSOR company_cur (id_in IN NUMBER)
    RETURN company%ROWTYPE;
    ```

This last example shows that the cursor can be declared separately from its implementation; for example, the header in a package specification and the implementation in the package body. See the "Packages" section for more information.

Opening explicit cursors

To open a cursor, use the following syntax:

```
OPEN cursor_name [(argument [,argument ...])];
```

where *cursor_name* is the name of the cursor as declared in the declaration section. The arguments are required if the definition of the cursor contains a parameter list.

You must open an explicit cursor before you can fetch rows from that cursor. When the cursor is opened, the processing actually includes the parse, bind, open, and execute phases of SQL statement execution. This OPEN processing includes determining an execution plan, associating host variables and cursor parameters with the placeholders in the SQL statement, determining the result set, and, finally, setting the current row pointer to the first row in the result set.

When using a cursor FOR loop, the OPEN is implicit in the FOR statement. If you try to open a cursor that is already open, PL/SQL will raise an "ORA-06511: PL/SQL: cursor already open" exception.

Fetching from explicit cursors

The FETCH statement places the contents of the current row into local variables. To retrieve all rows in a result set, each row needs to be fetched. The syntax for a FETCH statement is:

```
FETCH cursor_name INTO record_or_variable_list;
```

where *cursor_name* is the name of the cursor as declared and opened.

Closing explicit cursors

After all rows have been fetched, a cursor needs to be closed. Closing a cursor enables the PL/SQL memory optimization algorithm to release the associated memory at an appropriate time. You can close an explicit cursor by specifying a CLOSE statement as follows:

```
CLOSE cursor_name;
```

where *cursor_name* is the name of the cursor declared and opened.

If you declare a cursor in a local anonymous, procedure, or function block, that cursor will automatically close when the block terminates. Package-based cursors must be closed explicitly, or they stay open for the duration of your session. Closing a cursor that is not open raises an INVALID CURSOR exception.

Explicit cursor attributes

There are four attributes associated with cursors: ISOPEN, FOUND, NOTFOUND, and ROWCOUNT. These attributes can be accessed with the % delimiter to obtain information about the state of the cursor. The syntax for a cursor attribute is:

```
cursor_name%attribute
```

where *cursor_name* is the name of the explicit cursor.

The behaviors of the explicit cursor attributes are described in the following table:

Attribute	Description
%ISOPEN	TRUE if cursor is open. FALSE if cursor is not open.
%FOUND	INVALID_CURSOR is raised if cursor has not been OPENed. NULL before the first fetch. TRUE if record was fetched successfully. FALSE if no row was returned. INVALID_CURSOR if cursor has been CLOSEd.
%NOTFOUND	INVALID_CURSOR is raised if cursor has not been OPENed. NULL before the first fetch. FALSE if record was fetched successfully. TRUE if no row was returned. INVALID_CURSOR if cursor has been CLOSEd.
%ROWCOUNT	INVALID_CURSOR is raised if cursor has not been OPENed. The number of rows fetched from the cursor. INVALID_CURSOR if cursor has been CLOSEd.

Frequently, a cursor attribute is checked as part of a WHILE loop that fetches rows from a cursor, as shown here:

```
DECLARE
   caller_rec caller_pkg.caller_cur%ROWTYPE;
BEGIN
   OPEN caller_pkg.caller_cur;
   LOOP
      FETCH caller_pkg.caller_cur into caller_rec;
      EXIT WHEN caller_pkg.caller_cur%NOTFOUND
                OR
                caller_pkg.caller_cur%ROWCOUNT > 10;

      UPDATE call
         SET caller_id = caller_rec.caller_id
```

```
          WHERE call_timestamp < SYSDATE;
   END LOOP;
   CLOSE caller_pkg.caller_cur;
END;
```

Implicit Cursors

Whenever a SQL statement is directly in the execution or exception section of a PL/SQL block, you are working with implicit cursors. SQL statements handled this way include INSERT, UPDATE, DELETE, MERGE, and SELECT INTO. Unlike explicit cursors, implicit cursors do not need to be declared, OPENed, FETCHed, or CLOSEd.

SELECT statements handle the %FOUND and %NOTFOUND attributes differently from the way that explicit cursors do. When an implicit SELECT statement does not return any rows, PL/SQL immediately raises the NO_DATA_FOUND exception and control passes to the exception section. When an implicit SELECT returns more than one row, PL/SQL immediately raises the TOO_MANY_ROWS exception and control passes to the exception section.

Implicit cursor attributes are referenced via the SQL cursor. For example:

```
BEGIN
   UPDATE activity SET last_accessed := SYSDATE
   WHERE UID = user_id;

   IF SQL%NOTFOUND THEN
      INSERT INTO activity_log (uid,last_accessed)
      VALUES (user_id,SYSDATE);
   END IF
END;
```

The following table lists the implicit cursor attributes:

Attributes	Description
SQL%ISOPEN	Always FALSE because the cursor is opened implicitly and closed immediately after the statement is executed.

Attributes	Description
SQL%FOUND	NULL before the statement. TRUE if one or more rows were inserted, merged, updated, or deleted or if only one row was selected. FALSE if no row was selected, merged, updated, inserted, or deleted.
SQL%NOTFOUND	NULL before the statement. TRUE if no row was selected, merged, updated, inserted, or deleted. FALSE if one or more rows were inserted, merged, updated, or deleted.
SQL%ROWCOUNT	Number of rows affected by the cursor.
SQL%BULK_ROWCOUNT	Pseudo index-by table containing the numbers of rows affected by the statements executed in bulk bind operations. See the "Bulk Binds" section for more information. (Introduced with Oracle8*i*.)

Use the RETURNING clause in INSERT, UPDATE, and DELETE statements to obtain data modified by the associated DML statement. This clause allows you to avoid an additional SELECT statement to query the results of the DML statement. For example:

```
BEGIN
   UPDATE activity SET last_accessed := SYSDATE
   WHERE UID = user_id
   RETURNING last_accessed, cost_center
   INTO timestamp, chargeback_acct;
```

SELECT FOR UPDATE clause

By default, the Oracle RDBMS locks rows as they are changed. To lock all rows in a result set, use the FOR UPDATE clause in your SELECT statement when you OPEN the cursor, instead of when you change the data. Using the FOR UPDATE clause does not require you to actually make changes to the data; it only locks the rows when opening the cursor. These locks are released on the next COMMIT or ROLLBACK. As always, these row locks do not affect other SELECT statements unless they, too, are FOR UPDATE. The

FOR UPDATE clause is appended to the end of the SELECT statement and has the following syntax:

```
SELECT ...
  FROM ...
   FOR UPDATE [OF column_reference] [NOWAIT];
```

where *column_reference* is a comma-delimited list of columns that appear in the SELECT clause. The NOWAIT keyword tells the RDBMS to not wait for other blocking locks to be released. The default is to wait forever.

In the following example, only columns from the inventory (pet) table are referenced FOR UPDATE, so no rows in the dog_breeds (dog) table are locked when hounds_in_stock_cur is opened:

```
DECLARE
   CURSOR hounds_in_stock_cur IS
      SELECT pet.stock_no, pet.breeder, dog.size
        FROM dog_breeds dog ,inventory pet
       WHERE dog.breed = pet.breed
         AND dog.class = 'HOUND'
         FOR UPDATE OF pet.stock_no, pet.breeder;
BEGIN
```

WHERE CURRENT OF clause

UPDATE and DELETE statements can use a WHERE CURRENT OF clause if they reference a cursor declared FOR UPDATE. This syntax indicates that the UPDATE or DELETE should modify the current row identified by the FOR UPDATE cursor. The syntax is:

```
[UPDATE | DELETE ] ...
   WHERE CURRENT OF cursor_name;
```

By using WHERE CURRENT OF, you do not have to repeat the WHERE clause in the SELECT statement. For example:

```
DECLARE
   CURSOR wip_cur IS
      SELECT acct_no, enter_date FROM wip
       WHERE enter_date < SYSDATE - 7
         FOR UPDATE;
```

Cursors in PL/SQL | 39

```
BEGIN
   FOR wip_rec IN wip_cur
   LOOP
      INSERT INTO acct_log (acct_no, order_date)
         VALUES (wip_rec.acct_no, wip_rec.enter_
            date);
      DELETE FROM wip
         WHERE CURRENT OF wip_cur;
   END LOOP;
END;
```

Dynamic Cursors

Dynamic cursors are implemented with an EXECUTE IMMEDIATE statement together with the OPEN FOR, FETCH, and CLOSE statements. The EXECUTE IMMEDIATE statement supports single-row queries and DDL, while the OPEN FOR, FETCH, and CLOSE statements support dynamic multi-row queries. The syntax for these statements is:

```
EXECUTE IMMEDIATE sql_statement
   [INTO {variable [,variable ...] | record}]
   [USING [IN | OUT | IN OUT] bind_argument
     [,[IN | OUT | IN OUT] bind_argument ...] ]
   [{RETURNING | RETURN} INTO bind_argument
     [,bind_argument]...];
```

The EXECUTE IMMEDIATE statement parses and executes the SQL statement in a single step. The EXECUTE IMMEDIATE statement requires a terminating semicolon, but the *sql_statement* must not have a trailing semicolon. For example:

```
EXECUTE IMMEDIATE 'TRUNCATE TABLE foo';
EXECUTE IMMEDIATE 'GRANT SELECT ON '|| tabname_v ||
   ' TO ' || grantee_list;
```

The OPEN FOR statement assigns a multi-row query to a weakly typed cursor variable. The rows are then FETCHed and the cursor CLOSEd:

```
DECLARE
    TYPE cv_typ IS REF CURSOR;
    cv cv_typ;
    laccount_no NUMBER;
    lbalance NUMBER;
```

```
BEGIN
   OPEN cv FOR
      'SELECT account_no, balance
         FROM accounts
         WHERE balance < 500';
   LOOP
      FETCH cv INTO laccount_no, lbalance;
      EXIT WHEN cv%NOTFOUND;
      -- Process the row.
   END LOOP;
   CLOSE cv;
END;
```

Because SQL statements usually execute repeatedly, declare your dynamic cursor with bind variables and pass the values to Oracle at runtime. The parsed form of the statement can be reused from the shared pool, improving performance. For example:

```
EXECUTE IMMEDIATE 'INSERT INTO hr.regions
   (region_id, region_name) VALUES (:r_id, :r_name)'
   USING  id, name;
```

Cursor Variables

A *cursor variable* is a data structure that points to a cursor object, which in turn points to the cursor's result set. You can use cursor variables to more easily retrieve rows in a result set from client and server programs. You can also use cursor variables to hide minor variations in queries.

The syntax for a REF_CURSOR type (cursor variable) is:

```
TYPE ref_cursor_name IS REF CURSOR
   [RETURN record_type];
```

If you do not include a RETURN clause, then you are declaring a weak REF CURSOR. Cursor variables declared from weak REF CURSORs can be associated with any query at runtime. A REF CURSOR declaration with a RETURN clause defines a "strong" REF CURSOR. A cursor variable based on a strong REF CURSOR can be associated with queries whose result sets match the number and datatype of the record structure after the RETURN at runtime.

To use cursor variables, you must first create a REF_CURSOR type, then declare a cursor variable based on that type.

The following example shows the use of both weak and strong REF CURSORs:

```
DECLARE
   -- Create a cursor type based on the company's
      table.
   TYPE company_curtype IS REF CURSOR
      RETURN companies%ROWTYPE;

   -- Create the variable based on the REF CURSOR.
   company_cur company_curtype;

   -- And now the weak, general approach.
   TYPE any_curtype IS REF CURSOR;
   generic_curvar any_curtype;
```

The syntax to OPEN a cursor variable is:

```
OPEN cursor_name FOR SELECT_statement;
```

FETCH and CLOSE a cursor variable using the same syntax as for explicit cursors. There are a number of restrictions on cursor variables:

- You cannot declare package-level cursor variables because they do not have a persistent state. (You can declare them in packaged procedures and functions, however.)
- You cannot assign NULLs to a cursor variable nor can you use comparison operators to test for equality, inequality, or nullity.
- Neither database columns nor collections can store cursor variables.
- You cannot use RPCs to pass cursor variables from one server to another.

Cursor Expressions

A *cursor expression* is a cursor that is used as a column expression in the SELECT list of an explicit cursor. The syntax for a cursor expression is:

```
CURSOR (subquery)
```

Cursor expressions can reduce the amount of redundant data returned to a calling program over techniques that involve joining the tables together. The cursor expression is automatically opened when the parent row is fetched. Cursor expressions can be nested as well. These nested cursors are closed when one of the following occurs:

- The nested cursor is explicitly closed by the program.
- The parent cursor is closed.
- The parent cursor is re-executed.
- An exception is raised during the fetch of the parent row.

An example of a cursor expression follows:

```
DECLARE
TYPE refcursor IS REF CURSOR;
CURSOR order_cur IS
   SELECT o.order_date ,o.order_status
         ,CURSOR(SELECT p.translated_name
                       ,i.unit_price
                       ,i.quantity
                  FROM oe.order_items i
                       ,oe.product_descriptions p
                  WHERE i.product_id = p.product_id
                    AND i.order_id = o.order_id)
   FROM oe.orders o
   WHERE order_date BETWEEN TO_DATE('01-Jan-03')
                        AND TO_DATE('31-Jan_03');
odate   oe.orders.order_date%TYPE;
ostatus oe.orders.order_status%TYPE;
od_cur  refcursor;
tname   oe.product_descriptions.translated_name%TYPE;
price   oe.order_items.unit_price%TYPE;
qty     oe.order_items.quantity%TYPE;
BEGIN
   OPEN order_cur;
   LOOP
```

```
      FETCH order_cur INTO odate, ostatus, od_cur;
      EXIT WHEN order_cur%NOTFOUND;
      LOOP
         FETCH od_cur INTO tname, price, qty;
         EXIT WHEN od_cur%NOTFOUND;
         DBMS_OUTPUT.PUT_LINE(odate||','||ostatus
            ||','||tname||','||price||','||qty);
      END LOOP;
   END LOOP;
   CLOSE order_cur;
END;
```

Exception Handling

PL/SQL allows developers to raise and handle errors (exceptions) in a very flexible and powerful way. Each PL/SQL block can have its own exception section in which exceptions can be trapped and handled (resolved or passed on to the enclosing block).

When an exception occurs (is raised) in a PL/SQL block, its execution section immediately terminates. Control is passed to the exception section.

Every exception in PL/SQL has an error number and error message; some exceptions also have names.

Declaring Exceptions

Some exceptions (see the following table) have been predefined by Oracle in the STANDARD package or other built-in packages, such as UTL_FILE. You can also declare your own exceptions as follows:

```
DECLARE
    exception_name EXCEPTION;
```

Error	Named exception
ORA-00001	DUP_VAL_ON_INDEX
ORA-00051	TIMEOUT_ON_RESOURCE
ORA-00061	TRANSACTION_BACKED_OUT

Error	Named exception
ORA-01001	INVALID_CURSOR
ORA-01012	NOT_LOGGED_ON
ORA-01017	LOGIN_DENIED
ORA-01403	NO_DATA_FOUND
ORA-01410	SYS_INVALID_ROWID
ORA-01422	TOO_MANY_ROWS
ORA-01476	ZERO_DIVIDE
ORA-01725	USERENV_COMMMITSCN_ERROR
ORA-01722	INVALID_NUMBER
ORA-06500	STORAGE_ERROR
ORA-06501	PROGRAM_ERROR
ORA-06502	VALUE_ERROR
ORA-06504	ROWTYPE_MISMATCH
ORA-06511	CURSOR_ALREADY_OPEN
ORA-06530	ACCESS_INTO_NULL
ORA-06531	COLLECTION_IS_NULL
ORA-06532	SUBSCRIPT_OUTSIDE_LIMIT
ORA-06533	SUBSCRIPT_BEYOND_COUNT
ORA-09592	CASE_NOT_FOUND
ORA-30625	SELF_IS_NULL
ORA-29280	INVALID_PATH
ORA-29281	INVALID_MODE
ORA-29282	INVALID_FILEHANDLE
ORA-29283	INVALID_OPERATION
ORA-29284	READ_ERROR
ORA-29285	WRITE_ERROR
ORA-29286	INTERNAL_ERROR
ORA-29287	INVALID_MAXLINESIZE
ORA-29288	INVALID_FILENAME
ORA-29289	ACCESS_DENIED

Error	Named exception
ORA-29290	INVALID_OFFSET
ORA-29291	DELETE_FAILED
ORA-29292	RENAME_FAILED

An exception can be declared only once in a block, but nested blocks can declare an exception with the same name as an outer block. If this multiple declaration occurs, scope takes precedence over name when handling the exception. The inner block's declaration takes precedence over a global declaration.

When you declare your own exception, you must RAISE it explicitly. All declared exceptions have an error code of 1 and the error message "User-defined exception," unless you use the EXCEPTION_INIT pragma.

You can associate an error number with a declared exception with the PRAGMA EXCEPTION_INIT statement using the following syntax:

```
DECLARE
   exception_name EXCEPTION;
   PRAGMA EXCEPTION_INIT (exception_name,
      error_number);
```

where *error_number* is a literal value (variable references are not allowed). This number can be an Oracle error, such as -1855, or an error in the user-definable -20000 to -20999 range.

Raising Exceptions

An exception can be raised in three ways:

- By the PL/SQL runtime engine
- By an explicit RAISE statement in your code
- By a call to the built-in function RAISE_APPLICATION_ ERROR

The syntax for the RAISE statement is:

```
RAISE exception_name;
```

where *exception_name* is the name of an exception that you have declared, or an exception that is declared in the STANDARD package. If you use the RAISE statement inside an exception handler, you can omit the exception name to re-raise the current exception:

```
RAISE;
```

This syntax is not valid outside the exception section.

The RAISE_APPLICATION_ERROR built-in function has the following header:

```
RAISE_APPLICATION_ERROR (
    num BINARY_INTEGER,
    msg VARCHAR2,
    keeperrorstack BOOLEAN DEFAULT FALSE);
```

where *num* is the error number (an integer between -20999 and -20000), *msg* is the associated error message, and *keeperrorstack* controls the contents of the error stack.

Scope

The scope of an exception section is that portion of the code that is "covered" by the exception section. An exception handler will only handle or attempt to handle exceptions raised in the executable section of the PL/SQL block. Exceptions raised in the declaration or exception sections are automatically passed to the outer block. Any line or set of PL/SQL code can be placed inside its own block and given its own exception section. This allows you to limit the propagation of an exception.

Propagation

Exceptions raised in a PL/SQL block propagate to an outer block if they are unhandled or re-raised in the exception section. When an exception occurs, PL/SQL looks for an exception handler that checks for the exception (or is the WHEN OTHERS clause) in the current block. If a match is not found, then PL/SQL propagates the exception to the enclosing block or calling program. This propagation continues until the exception is handled or propagated out of the outermost block, back to the calling program. In this case, the exception is "unhandled" and (1) stops the calling program, and (2) causes an automatic rollback of any outstanding transactions.

Once an exception is handled, it will not propagate upward. If you want to trap an exception, display a meaningful error message, and have the exception propagate upward as an error, you must re-raise the exception. The RAISE statement can re-raise the current exception or raise a new exception, as shown here:

```
PROCEDURE delete_dept(deptno_in IN NUMBER)
DECLARE
   still_have_employees EXCEPTION
   PRAGMA EXCEPTION_INIT(still_have_employees.
      -2292)
BEGIN
DELETE FROM dept
WHERE deptno = deptno_in;
EXCEPTION
   WHEN still_have_employees
   THEN
      DBMS_OUTPUT.PUT_LINE
('Please delete employees in dept first');
   ROLLBACK;
   RAISE;   /* Re-raise the current exception. */
END;
```

WHEN OTHERS clause

Use the WHEN OTHERS clause in the exception handler as a catch-all to trap any exceptions that are not handled by specific WHEN clauses in the exception section. If present, this clause must be the last exception handler in the exception section. You specify this clause as follows:

```
EXCEPTION
   WHEN OTHERS
   THEN
      ...
```

SQLCODE and SQLERRM

SQLCODE and SQLERRM are built-in functions that provide the SQL error code and message for the current exception. Use these functions inside the exception section's WHEN OTHERS clause to handle specific errors by number. The EXCEPTION_INIT pragma allows you to handle errors by name. For example, the following code:

```
CREATE TABLE err_test
   (widget_name   VARCHAR2(100)
   ,widget_count  NUMBER
   ,CONSTRAINT no_small_numbers CHECK
      (widget_count > 1000));
BEGIN
   INSERT INTO err_test (widget_name, widget_count)
   VALUES ('Athena',2);
EXCEPTION
   WHEN OTHERS THEN
   IF SQLCODE = -2290
      AND SQLERRM LIKE '%NO_SMALL_NUMBERS%'
   THEN
      DBMS_OUTPUT.PUT_LINE('widget_count is too
         small');
   ELSE
      DBMS_OUTPUT.PUT_LINE('Exception not handled,'
         ||'SQLcode='||SQLCODE);
      DBMS_OUTPUT.PUT_LINE(SQLERRM);
   END IF;
END;
```

produces this output:

```
widget_count is too small
```

The built-in package DBMS_UTILITY's FORMAT_ERROR_STACK and FORMAT_CALL_STACK procedures can be used to capture the full error stack and call stack. See the book *Oracle Built-in Packages* for more information on DBMS_UTILITY.

Exceptions and DML

When an exception is raised in a PL/SQL block, it does *not* roll back your current transaction, even if the block itself issued an INSERT, UPDATE, or DELETE. You must issue your own ROLLBACK statement if you want to clean up your transaction as a result of the exception.

If your exception goes unhandled (propagates out of the outermost block), however, most host environments will then force an automatic, unqualified rollback of any outstanding changes in your session.

Records in PL/SQL

A PL/SQL record is a data structure composed of multiple pieces of information called *fields*. To use a record, you must first define it and declare a variable of this type.

There are three types of records: table-based, cursor-based, and programmer-defined.

Declaring Records

You define and declare records either in the declaration section of a PL/SQL block or globally, via a package specification.

You do not have to explicitly define table-based or cursor-based records, as they are implicitly defined with the same structure as a table or a cursor. Variables of these types are declared via the %ROWTYPE attribute. The record's fields correspond to the table's columns or the columns in the SELECT list. For example:

```
DECLARE
   -- Declare table-based record for company table.
   comp_rec   company%ROWTYPE

   CURSOR comp_summary_cur IS
      SELECT C.company_id,SUM(S.gross_sales) gross
```

```
    FROM company C ,sales S
    WHERE C.company_id = S.company_id;

-- Declare a cursor-based record.
comp_summary_rec    comp_summary_cur%ROWTYPE;
```

Programmer-defined records must be explicitly defined with the TYPE statement in the PL/SQL declaration section or in a package specification. Variables of this type can then be declared as shown here:

```
DECLARE
    TYPE name_rectype IS RECORD(
        prefix       VARCHAR2(15)
        ,first_name  VARCHAR2(30)
        ,middle_name VARCHAR2(30)
        ,sur_name    VARCHAR2(30)
        ,suffix      VARCHAR2(10) );

    TYPE employee_rectype IS RECORD (
        emp_id       NUMBER(10) NOT NULL
        ,mgr_id      NUMBER(10)
        ,dept_no     dept.deptno%TYPE
        ,title       VARCHAR2(20)
        ,name        empname_rectype
        ,hire_date   DATE := SYSDATE
        ,fresh_out   BOOLEAN );

    -- Declare a variable of this type.
    new_emp_rec employee_rectype;
BEGIN
```

Referencing Fields of Records

Individual fields are referenced via dot notation:

record_name.field_name

For example:

```
employee.first_name
```

Individual fields within a record can be read from or written to. They can appear on either the left or right side of the assignment operator:

Records in PL/SQL | 51

```
BEGIN
   insurance_start_date := new_emp_rec.hire_date +
      30;
   new_emp_rec.fresh_out := FALSE;
   ...
```

Record Assignment

An entire record can be assigned to another record of the same type, but one record cannot be compared to another record via Boolean operators. This is a valid assignment:

```
shipto_address_rec := customer_address_rec
```

This is not a valid comparison:

```
IF shipto_address_rec = customer_address_rec
THEN
   ...
END IF;
```

The individual fields of the records need to be compared instead.

Values can be assigned to records or to the fields within a record in four different ways:

- The assignment operator can be used to assign a value to a field:

    ```
    new_emp_rec.hire_date := SYSDATE;
    ```

- You can SELECT INTO a whole record or the individual fields:

    ```
    SELECT emp_id,dept,title,hire_date,college_recruit
      INTO new_emp_rec
      FROM emp
     WHERE surname = 'LI'
    ```

- You can FETCH INTO a whole record or the individual fields:

    ```
    FETCH emp_cur INTO new_emp_rec;
    FETCH emp_cur INTO new_emp_rec.emp_id,
       new_emp_rec.name;
    ```

- You can assign all of the fields of one record variable to another record variable of the same type:

  ```
  IF rehire THEN
    new_emp_rec := former_emp_rec;
  ENDIF;
  ```

  This aggregate assignment technique works only for records declared with the same TYPE statement.

Nested Records

Nested records are records contained in fields that are records themselves. Nesting records is a powerful way to normalize data structures and hide complexity within PL/SQL programs. For example:

```
DECLARE
   -- Define a record.
   TYPE phone_rectype IS RECORD (
      area_code   VARCHAR2(3),
      exchange    VARCHAR2(3),
      phn_number  VARCHAR2(4),
      extension   VARCHAR2(4));

   -- Define a record composed of records.
   TYPE contact_rectype IS RECORD (
      day_phone#   phone_rectype,
      eve_phone#   phone_rectype,
      cell_phone#  phone_rectype);

-- Declare a variable for the nested record.
 auth_rep_info_rec contact_rectype;
BEGIN
```

Named Program Units

PL/SQL allows you to create a variety of named program units, or containers for code. These include:

Procedure
   A program that executes one or more statements

Function
   A program that returns a value

Package
    A container for procedures, functions, and data structures

Trigger
    A program that executes in response to database changes

Object type
    Oracle's version of an object-oriented class; object types can contain member procedures and functions

Procedures

Procedures are program units that execute one or more statements and can receive or return zero or more values through their parameter lists. The syntax of a procedure is:

```
CREATE [OR REPLACE] PROCEDURE name
   [ (parameter [,parameter]) ]
   [AUTHID { CURRENT_USER | DEFINER } ]
   [DETERMINISTIC]
{ IS | AS }
   declaration_section
BEGIN
   executable_section
[EXCEPTION
   exception_section]
END [name];
```

A procedure is called as a standalone executable PL/SQL statement:

```
apply_discount(new_company_id, 0.15);
```

Functions

Functions are program units that execute zero or more statements and return a value through the RETURN clause. Functions can also receive or return zero or more values through their parameter lists. The syntax of a function is:

```
CREATE [OR REPLACE] FUNCTION name
   [ (parameter [,parameter]) ]
   RETURN return_datatype
```

```
   [AUTHID { CURRENT_USER | DEFINER } ]
   [DETERMINISTIC]
   [PARALLEL_ENABLE]
   [PIPELINED]
   [AGGREGATE USING]
{ IS | AS }
   [declaration_section]
BEGIN
   executable_section
[EXCEPTION
   exception_section]
END [name];
```

A function must have at least one RETURN statement in the execution section. The RETURN clause in the function header specifies the datatype of the returned value.

See the "Compiling stored PL/SQL programs" section for information on the keywords OR REPLACE, AUTHID, DETERMINISTIC, PARALLEL_ENABLE, PIPELINED, and AGGREGATE USING. See the upcoming "Privileges and stored PL/SQL" section for additional information on AUTHID.

A function can be called anywhere that an expression of the same type can be used. You can call a function:

- In an assignment statement:

    ```
    sales95 := tot_sales(1995,'C');
    ```

- To set a default value:

    ```
    DECLARE
        sales95 NUMBER DEFAULT tot_sales(1995,'C');
    BEGIN
    ```

- In a Boolean expression:

    ```
    IF tot_sales(1995,'C') > 10000
    THEN
    ...
    ```

- In a SQL statement:

    ```
    SELECT first_name ,surname
        FROM sellers
    WHERE tot_sales(1995,'C') > 1000;
    ```

- As an argument in another program unit's parameter list.

Named Program Units | **55**

Here, for example, max_discount is a programmer-defined function and SYSDATE is a built-in function:

```
apply_discount(company_id, max_discount(SYSDATE));
```

Parameters

Procedures, functions, and cursors may have a parameter list. This list contains one or more parameters that allow you to pass information back and forth between the sub-program and the calling program. Each parameter is defined by its name, datatype, mode, and optional default value. The syntax for a parameter is:

```
parameter_name [mode] [NOCOPY] datatype
   [ { := | DEFAULT } value]
```

Datatype

The datatype can be any PL/SQL or programmer-defined datatype, but cannot be constrained by a size (NUMBER is valid, NUMBER(10) is not valid). The actual size of the parameter is determined from the calling program or via a %TYPE constraint.

```
CREATE OR REPLACE PROCEDURE empid_to_name
(in_id            emp.emp_id%TYPE -- Compiles OK.
,out_last_name    VARCHAR2        -- Compiles OK.
,out_first_name   VARCHAR2(10)    -- Won't compile.
) IS
...
```

The lengths of out_last_name and out_first_name are determined by the calling program:

```
DECLARE
   surname      VARCHAR2(10);
   first_name   VARCHAR2(10);
BEGIN
   empid_to_name(10, surname, first_name);
END;
```

Mode

The mode of a parameter specifies whether the parameter can be read from or written to, as shown in the following table:

Mode	Description	Parameter usage
IN	Read-only	The value of the actual parameter can be referenced inside the program, but the parameter cannot be changed.
OUT or IN OUT	Read/write	The program can both reference (read) and modify (write) the parameter.

If the mode is not explicitly defined, it defaults to IN.

OUT parameters are not the same as IN OUT parameters. When running the called program, the runtime engine ignores (sets to NULL) any argument value you supply for an OUT parameter; it preserves the value provided for an IN OUT. If an exception is raised during execution of a procedure or function, assignments made to OUT or IN OUT parameters get rolled back unless the parameter includes the NOCOPY option.

The NOCOPY compiler hint for parameters makes the parameter a call by reference instead of a call by value. Normally, PL/SQL passes IN/OUT parameters by value—a copy of the parameter is created for the sub-program. When parameter items get large, as collections and objects do, the copy can eat memory and slow down processing. NOCOPY directs PL/SQL to pass the parameter by reference, using a pointer to the single copy of the parameter.

The disadvantage of NOCOPY is that when an exception is raised during execution of a program that has modified an OUT or IN OUT parameter, the changes to the actual parameters are not "rolled back" because the parameters were passed by reference instead of being copied.

Default values

IN parameters can be given default values. If an IN parameter has a default value, then you do not need to supply an argument for that parameter when you call the program unit. It automatically uses the default value. For example:

```
CREATE OR REPLACE PROCEDURE hire_employee
   (emp_id      IN VARCHAR2
   ,hire_date   IN DATE := SYSDATE
   ,company_id  IN NUMBER := 1
   )
IS
   ...
```

Here are some example calls to the above procedure:

```
-- Use two default values.
hire_employee(new_empno);
-- Use one default value.
hire_employee(new_empno,'12-Jan-1999');
-- Use non-trailing default value, named notation.
hire_employee(emp_id=>new_empno, comp_id=>12);
```

Parameter-passing notations

Formal parameters are the names that are declared in the header of a procedure or function. *Actual parameters* (*arguments*) are the values or expressions placed in the parameter list when a procedure or function is called. In the empid_to_name example shown earlier in the "Datatype" section, the actual parameters to the procedure are in_id, out_last_name, and out_first_name. The formal parameters used in the call to this procedure are 10, surname, and first_name.

PL/SQL lets you use either of two styles for passing arguments in parameter lists: positional notation or named notation.

Positional notation
   The default. Each value in the list of arguments supplied in the program call is associated with the parameter in the corresponding position.

Named notation
> Explicitly associates the argument value with its parameter by name (not position). When you use named notation, you can supply the arguments in any order and you can omit IN arguments that have default values.

The call to the empid_to_name procedure is shown here with both notations:

```
BEGIN
   -- Implicit positional notation.
   empid_to_name(10, surname, first_name);

   -- Explicit named notation.
   empid_to_name(in_id=>10
      ,out_last_name=>surname
      ,out_first_name=>first_name);
END;
```

You may combine positional and named notation, as long as positional arguments appear to the left of any named notation arguments; for example:

```
empid_to_name(10, surname, out_first_name => first_name);
```

When calling stored functions from SQL, named notation is not supported.

Local programs

A local program is a procedure or function that is defined in the declaration section of a PL/SQL block. The declaration of a local program must appear at the end of the declaration section, after the declarations of any types, records, cursors, variables, and exceptions. A program defined in a declaration section may only be referenced within that block's executable and exception sections. It is not defined outside that block.

The following program defines a local procedure and function:

```
PROCEDURE track_revenue
IS
```

```
   l_total NUMBER;

   PROCEDURE calc_total (year_in IN INTEGER) IS
   BEGIN
      calculations here ...
   END;

   FUNCTION below_minimum (comp_id IN INTEGER)
      RETURN BOOLEAN
   IS
   BEGIN
      ...
   END;
BEGIN
   ...main procedure logic here
END;
```

Local programs may be overloaded with the same restrictions as overloaded packaged programs.

Program overloading

PL/SQL allows you to define two or more programs with the same name within any declaration section, including a package specification or body. This is called *overloading*. If two or more programs have the same name, they must be different in some other way so that the compiler can determine which program should be used.

Here is an example of overloaded programs in a built-in package specification:

```
PACKAGE DBMS_OUTPUT
IS
   PROCEDURE PUT_LINE (a VARCHAR2);
   PROCEDURE PUT_LINE (a NUMBER);
   PROCEDURE PUT_LINE (a DATE);
END;
```

Each PUT_LINE procedure is identical, except for the datatype of the parameter. That is enough difference for the compiler.

To overload programs successfully, one or more of the following conditions must be true:

- Parameters must differ by datatype family (number, character, datetime, or Boolean).
- The program type must be different (you can overload a function and a procedure of the same name and identical parameter list).
- The numbers of parameters must be different.

You *cannot* overload programs if:

- Only the datatypes of the functions' RETURN clauses are different.
- Parameter datatypes are within the same family (CHAR and VARCHAR2, NUMBER and INTEGER, etc.).
- Only the modes of the parameters are different.

Forward declarations

Programs must be declared before they can be used. PL/SQL supports *mutual recursion*, in which program A calls program B, whereupon program B calls program A. To implement this mutual recursion, you must use a *forward declaration* of the programs. This technique declares a program in advance of the program definition, thus making it available for other programs to use. The forward declaration is the program header up to the IS/AS keyword:

```
PROCEDURE perform_calc(year_in IN NUMBER)
IS
   /* Forward declaration for total_cost
      function. */
   FUNCTION total_cost (...) RETURN NUMBER;

   /* The net_profit function can now use
      total_cost. */
   FUNCTION net_profit(...) RETURN NUMBER
   IS
   BEGIN
      RETURN total_sales(...) - total_cost(...);
   END;
```

```
   /* The Total_cost function calls net_profit. */
   FUNCTION total_cost (...) RETURN NUMBER
   IS
   BEGIN
      IF net_profit(...) < 0
      THEN
         RETURN 0;
         ELSE
         RETURN...;
      END IF;
   END;
BEGIN /* procedure perform_calc */
   ...
END perform_calc;
```

Table functions

Table functions take a collection or REF CURSOR (set of rows) as input and return a collection of records (set of rows) as output. The PIPE ROW command is used to identify the input and output streams. This streamlined nature allows you to pipeline table functions together, eliminating the need to stage tables between transformations. Table functions typically appear in the FROM clause of SQL statements. For example:

```
CREATE FUNCTION pet_family
(dad_in IN pet_t, mom_in IN pet_t)
RETURN pet_nt PIPELINED IS
   l_count PLS_INTEGER;
   retval pet_nt := pet_nt ( );

BEGIN
   PIPE ROW (dad_in);  -- identify streaming input
   PIPE ROW (mom_in);  -- identify streaming input

   IF mom_in.breed = 'RABBIT' THEN l_count := 12;
   ELSIF mom_in.breed = 'DOG' THEN l_count := 4;
   ELSIF mom_in.breed = 'KANGAROO' THEN l_count := 1;
   END IF;

   FOR indx IN 1 .. l_count
   LOOP
      -- stream the results into the ouput pipeline
      PIPE ROW (pet_t ('BABY' || indx, mom_in.breed
```

```
                        ,SYSDATE));
    END LOOP;

    RETURN;
END;
```

Compiling stored PL/SQL programs

The following keywords are available when creating Oracle9*i* stored programs:

OR REPLACE
　　Used to rebuild an existing program unit, preserving privileges granted on it.

AUTHID
　　Defines whether the program will execute with the privileges of, and resolve names like, the object owner (DEFINER), or as the user executing the function (CURRENT_USER). Prior to Oracle8*i*, only the built-in packages DBMS_SQL and DBMS_UTILITY executed as CURRENT_USER. The default AUTHID is DEFINER.

DETERMINISTIC
　　Required for function-based indexes. A function is DETERMINISTIC if it always returns the same value when called with the same parameters. Deterministic functions do not meaningfully reference package variables or the database. The built-in INITCAP is deterministic, but SYSDATE is not.

PARALLEL_ENABLED [(PARTITION in_parm BY {ANY HASH | RANGE})]
　　Tells the optimizer that a function is safe for parallel execution. The PARTITION BY clause is only available to functions that have a REF CURSOR IN parameter. This clause is used with table functions and tells the optimizer how the input can be partitioned.

PIPELINED (Oracle9i)
　　Used with table functions. Specifies that the results of this table function should be returned iteratively via the

PIPE ROW command. A pipelined function can start to return data as it is generated instead of all at once after processing is complete.

AGGREGATE USING (Oracle9i)
Required for aggregate functions. Tells Oracle that the function evaluates a group of rows and returns a single result. For example, the built-in function AVG is an aggregate function.

Native compilation of PL/SQL (Oracle9i)

With Oracle9*i* you can speed up many of your PL/SQL programs by compiling the stored programs natively. Oracle will translate your PL/SQL program into C code and compile it into a shared library (DLL on NT). You must have a supported C compiler on your database server machine to use native compilation. To compile natively, you must follow these steps:

- Edit the makefile, *spnc_makefile.mk*, which you should find in the *$ORACLE_HOME/plsql* subdirectory.
- Set the initialization parameter PLSQL_COMPILER_FLAGS = 'NATIVE'. Individual developers may alter the value of PLSQL_COMPILER_FLAGS using the ALTER SESSION statement.
- The following parameters many also need to be set: PLSQL_NATIVE_C_COMPILER, PLSQL_NATIVE_LINKER, PLSQL_NATIVE_LIBRARY_DIR, PLSQL_NATIVE_MAKE_UTILITY, and PLSQL_NATIVE_MAKE_FILE_NAME. The DBA can set these parameters in the Oracle initialization file or using an ALTER SYSTEM statement.
- Create or replace your stored programs.
- Verify the native compilation by querying the data dictionary view USER_STORED_SETTINGS and also by locating the shared library or DLL in the database server's file system.

Privileges and stored PL/SQL

Stored SQL supports two models for addressing privileges at runtime. The default is definer rights, which tells Oracle that the privileges of the owner or definer of the program should be used. With the definer rights model, the owner of the program must have the required privileges granted directly to him—he cannot inherit the privileges from a role.

With invoker rights, the user who executes the program does so using his own privileges. Anonymous PL/SQL blocks always execute with invoker rights. To create a program that uses the invoker rights model, include the keywords AUTHID CURRENT_USER in your program's declaration.

Triggers

Triggers are programs that execute in response to changes in table data or certain database events. There is a predefined set of events that can be "hooked" with a trigger, enabling you to integrate your own processing with that of the database. A triggering event *fires* or executes the trigger.

There are three types of triggering events:

- DML events fire when an INSERT, UPDATE, or DELETE statement executes.
- DDL events fire when a CREATE, ALTER, or DROP statement executes.
- Database events fire when one of the predefined database-level events occurs.

Complete lists of these events are included in later sections.

Creating Triggers

The syntax for creating a trigger on a DML event is:

```
CREATE [OR REPLACE] TRIGGER trigger_name
{ BEFORE | AFTER | INSTEAD OF } trigger_event
```

```
    ON {table_or_view_reference |
       NESTED TABLE nested_table_column OF view}
      [REFERENCING [OLD AS old] [NEW AS new]
         [PARENT AS parent]]
    [FOR EACH ROW ][WHEN trigger_condition]
    trigger_body;
```

The syntax for creating a trigger on a DDL or database event is:

```
CREATE [OR REPLACE] TRIGGER trigger_name
{ BEFORE | AFTER } trigger_event
   ON [ DATABASE | schema ]
 [WHEN trigger_condition]
 trigger_body;
```

Trigger events are listed in the following table:

Trigger event	Description
INSERT	Fires whenever a row is added to the *table_or_view_reference*.
UPDATE	Fires whenever an UPDATE changes the *table_or_view_reference*. UPDATE triggers can additionally specify an OF clause to restrict firing to updates OF certain columns.
DELETE	Fires whenever a row is deleted from the *table_or_view_reference*. Does not fire on a TRUNCATE of the table.
ALTER	Fires whenever an ALTER statement changes a database object. In this context, objects are things like tables or packages (found in ALL_OBJECTS). Can apply to a single schema or the entire database.
DROP	Fires whenever a DROP statement removes an object from the database. In this context, objects are things like tables or packages (found in ALL_OBJECTS). Can apply to a single schema or the entire database.
SERVERERROR	Fires whenever a server error message is logged. Only AFTER triggers are allowed in this context.
LOGON	Fires whenever a session is created (a user connects to the database). Only AFTER triggers are allowed in this context.
LOGOFF	Fires whenever a session is terminated (a user disconnects from the database). Only BEFORE triggers are allowed in this context.
STARTUP	Fires when the database is opened. Only AFTER triggers are allowed in this context.
SHUTDOWN	Fires when the database is closed. Only BEFORE triggers are allowed in this context.

Triggers can fire BEFORE or AFTER the triggering event. AFTER data triggers are slightly more efficient than BEFORE triggers.

The REFERENCING clause is allowed only for the data events INSERT, UPDATE, and DELETE. It lets you give a non-default name to the old and new pseudo-records. These pseudo-records give the program visibility to the pre- and post-change values in row-level triggers. These records are defined like %ROWTYPE records, except that columns of type LONG or LONG RAW cannot be referenced. They are prefixed with a colon in the trigger body, and referenced with dot notation. Unlike other records, these fields can only be assigned individually—aggregate assignment is not allowed. All old fields are NULL within INSERT triggers, and all new fields are NULL within DELETE triggers.

FOR EACH ROW defines the trigger to be a row-level trigger. Row-level triggers fire once for each row affected. The default is a statement-level trigger, which fires only once for each triggering statement.

The WHEN *trigger_condition* specifies the conditions that must be met for the trigger to fire. Stored functions and object methods are not allowed in the trigger condition.

The trigger body is a standard PL/SQL block. For example:

```
CREATE OR REPLACE TRIGGER add_tstamp
   BEFORE INSERT ON emp
   REFERENCING NEW as new_row
   FOR EACH ROW
   BEGIN
      -- Automatically timestamp the entry.
      SELECT CURRENT_TIMESTAMP
      INTO :new_row.entry_timestamp
      FROM dual;
END add_tstamp;
```

Triggers are enabled on creation, and can be disabled (so they do not fire) with an ALTER statement, issued with the following syntax:

```
ALTER TRIGGER trigger_name { ENABLE | DISABLE };

ALTER TABLE table_name { ENABLE | DISABLE } ALL
   TRIGGERS;
```

Trigger Predicates

When using a single trigger for multiple events, use the trigger predicates INSERTING, UPDATING, and DELETING in the trigger condition to identify the triggering event, as shown in this example:

```
CREATE OR REPLACE TRIGGER emp_log_t
   AFTER INSERT OR UPDATE OR DELETE ON emp
   FOR EACH ROW
DECLARE
   dmltype  CHAR(1);
BEGIN
   IF INSERTING THEN
       dmltype := 'I';
       INSERT INTO emp_log (emp_no, who, operation)
           VALUES (:new.empno, USER, dmltype);
   ELSIF UPDATING  THEN
       dmltype := 'U';
       INSERT INTO emp_log (emp_no, who, operation)
           VALUES (:new.empno, USER, dmltype);
   END IF;
END;
```

DML Events

The DML events include INSERT, UPDATE, and DELETE statements on a table or view. Triggers on these events can be statement-level triggers (table only) or row-level triggers and can fire BEFORE or AFTER the triggering event. BEFORE triggers can modify the data in affected rows, but perform an additional logical read. AFTER triggers do not perform this additional logical read, and therefore perform slightly better, but are not able to change the *:new* values. AFTER triggers are thus better suited for data validation functionality. Triggers cannot be created on SYS-owned objects. The order in which these triggers fire, if present, is as follows:

> BEFORE statement-level trigger
> For each row affected by the statement:
> > BEFORE row-level trigger
> > The triggering statement
> > AFTER row-level trigger
>
> AFTER statement-level trigger

DDL Events

The DDL events are CREATE, ALTER, and DROP. These triggers fire whenever the respective DDL statement is executed. DDL triggers can apply to either a single schema or the entire database.

Database Events

The database events are SERVERERROR, LOGON, LOGOFF, STARTUP, and SHUTDOWN. Only BEFORE triggers are allowed for LOGOFF and SHUTDOWN events. Only AFTER triggers are allowed for LOGON, STARTUP, and SERVERERROR events. A SHUTDOWN trigger will fire on a SHUTDOWN NORMAL and a SHUTDOWN IMMEDIATE, but not on a SHUTDOWN ABORT.

Packages

A *package* is a collection of PL/SQL objects that are grouped together. There are a number of benefits to using packages, including information hiding, object-oriented design, top-down design, object persistence across transactions, and improved performance.

Elements that can be placed in a package include procedures, functions, constants, variables, cursors, exception names, and TYPE statements (for associative arrays [formerly known as index-by tables], records, REF CURSORs, etc.).

Package Structure

A package can have two parts: the specification and the body. The *package specification* is required and lists all the objects that are publicly available (i.e., may be referenced from outside the package) for use in applications. It also provides all the information a developer needs in order to use objects in the package; essentially, it is the package's API.

The *package body* contains all the code needed to implement procedures, functions, and cursors listed in the specification, as well as any private objects (accessible only to other elements defined in that package), and an optional initialization section.

If a package specification does not contain any procedures or functions and no private code is needed, then that package does not need to have a package body.

The syntax for the package specification is:

```
CREATE [OR REPLACE] PACKAGE package_name
[ AUTHID { CURRENT_USER | DEFINER } ]
{ IS | AS }

   [definitions of public TYPEs
   ,declarations of public variables, types, and
      objects
   ,declarations of exceptions
   ,pragmas
   ,declarations of cursors, procedures, and
      functions
   ,headers of procedures and functions]

END [package_name];
```

The syntax for the package body is:

```
CREATE [OR REPLACE] PACKAGE BODY package_name
   { IS | AS }

   [definitions of private TYPEs
   ,declarations of private variables, types, and
      objects
```

```
    ,full definitions of cursors
    ,full definitions of procedures and functions]

[BEGIN
   executable_statements

[EXCEPTION
   exception_handlers ] ]

END [package_name];
```

The optional OR REPLACE keywords are used to rebuild an existing package, preserving any EXECUTE privileges previously granted to other accounts. The declarations in the specifications cannot be repeated in the body. Both the executable section and the exception section are optional in a package body. If the executable section is present, it is called the *initialization section* and it executes only once—the first time any package element is referenced during a session.

You must compile the package specification before the body specification. When you grant EXECUTE authority on a package to another schema or to PUBLIC, you are giving access only to the specification; the body remains hidden.

Here's an example of a package:

```
CREATE OR REPLACE PACKAGE time_pkg IS
   FUNCTION  GetTimestamp  RETURN DATE;
   PRAGMA RESTRICT_REFERENCES (GetTimestamp, WNDS);

   PROCEDURE ResetTimestamp(new_time DATE DEFAULT
      SYSDATE);
END time_pkg;

CREATE OR REPLACE PACKAGE BODY time_pkg IS
   StartTimeStamp    DATE := SYSDATE;
   -- StartTimeStamp is package data.

   FUNCTION GetTimestamp RETURN DATE IS
   BEGIN
      RETURN StartTimeStamp;
   END GetTimestamp;
```

```
   PROCEDURE ResetTimestamp(new_time DATE DEFAULT SYSDATE)
   IS
   BEGIN
      StartTimeStamp := new_time;
   END ResetTimestamp;

END time_pkg;
```

Referencing Package Elements

The elements declared in the specification are referenced from the calling application via dot notation:

```
package_name.package_element
```

For example, the built-in package DBMS_OUTPUT has a procedure PUT_LINE, so a call to this package would look like this:

```
DBMS_OUTPUT.PUT_LINE('This is parameter data');
```

Package Data

Data structures declared within a package specification or body, but outside any procedure or function in the package, are *package data*. The scope of package data is your entire session, spanning transaction boundaries and acting as globals for your programs.

Keep the following guidelines in mind as you work with package data:

- The state of your package variables is not affected by COMMITs and ROLLBACKs.
- A cursor declared in a package has global scope. It remains OPEN until you close it explicitly or until your session ends.
- A good practice is to *hide* your data structures in the package body and provide "get and set" programs to read and write that data. This technique can help protect your data.

SERIALLY_REUSABLE Pragma

If you need package data to exist only during a call to the packaged functions or procedures, and not between calls of the current session, you can potentially save runtime memory by using the pragma SERIALLY_REUSABLE. After each call, PL/SQL closes the cursors and releases the memory used in the package. This technique is applicable only to large user communities executing the same routine. Normally, the database server's memory requirements grow linearly with the number of users; with SERIALLY_REUSABLE, this growth can be less than linear, because work areas for package states are kept in a pool in the Oracle's System Global Area (SGA) and are shared among all users. This pragma must appear in both the specification and the body, as shown here:

```
CREATE OR REPLACE PACKAGE my_pkg IS
   PRAGMA SERIALLY_REUSABLE;
   PROCEDURE foo;
END my_pkg;

CREATE OR REPLACE PACKAGE BODY my_pkg IS
   PRAGMA SERIALLY_REUSABLE;
   PROCEDURE foo IS
   ...
END my_pkg;
```

Package Initialization

The first time a user references a package element, the entire package is loaded into the SGA of the database instance to which the user is connected. That code is then shared by all sessions that have EXECUTE authority on the package.

Any package data are then instantiated into the session's User Global Area (UGA), a private area in either the System Global Area or the Program Global Area (PGA). If the package body contains an initialization section, that code will be executed. The initialization section is optional and appears at the end of the package body, beginning with a BEGIN statement and ending with the EXCEPTION section (if present) or the END of the package.

The following package initialization section runs a query to transfer the user's minimum balance into a global package variable. Programs can then reference the packaged variable (via the function) to retrieve the balance, rather than execute the query repeatedly:

```
CREATE OR REPLACE PACKAGE usrinfo
IS
   FUNCTION minbal RETURN VARCHAR2;
END usrinfo;
/

CREATE OR REPLACE PACKAGE BODY usrinfo
IS
   g_minbal NUMBER; -- Package data
   FUNCTION minbal RETURN VARCHAR2
      IS BEGIN RETURN g_minbal; END;
BEGIN  -- Initialization section
   SELECT minimum_balance
      INTO g_minbal
      FROM user_configuration
      WHERE username = USER;
EXCEPTION
   WHEN NO_DATA_FOUND
   THEN g_minbal := NULL;
END usrinfo;
```

Calling PL/SQL Functions in SQL

Stored functions can be called from SQL statements in a manner similar to built-in functions like DECODE, NVL, or RTRIM. This is a powerful technique for incorporating business rules into SQL in a simple and elegant way. Unfortunately, there are a number of caveats and restrictions.

The most notable caveat is that stored functions executed from SQL are not by default guaranteed to follow the statement-level read consistency model of the database. Unless the SQL statement and any stored functions in that statement are in the same read-consistent transaction (even if they are read-only), each execution of the stored function may look at a different time-consistent set of data. To avoid this potential problem, you need to ensure read consistency programmatically by issuing the SET TRANSACTION READ ONLY or SET TRANSACTION ISOLATION LEVEL SERIALIZABLE statement before executing your SQL statement containing the stored function. A COMMIT or ROLLBACK then needs to follow the SQL statement to end this read-consistent transaction.

Calling a Function

The syntax for calling a stored function from SQL is the same as that used to reference it from PL/SQL:

```
[schema_name.][pkg_name.]func_name[@db_link]
    [parm_list]
```

schema_name is optional and refers to the user/owner of the function or package. *pkg_name* is optional and refers to the package containing the called function. *func_name* is required and is the function name. *db_link* is optional and refers to the database link name to the remote database containing the function. *parm_list* is optional, as are the parameters passed to the function.

The following are example calls to the GetTimestamp function in the time_pkg example seen earlier in the "Package Structure" section:

```
-- Capture system events.
INSERT INTO v_sys_event (timestamp ,event ,qty_waits)
    SELECT time_pkg.GetTimestamp ,event ,total_waits
    FROM v$system_event

-- Capture system statistics.
INSERT INTO v_sys_stat (timestamp,stat#,value)
    SELECT time_pkg.GetTimestamp ,statistic# ,value
    FROM v$sysstat;
```

Requirements and Restrictions

There are a number of requirements for calling stored functions in SQL:

- All parameters must be IN; no IN OUT or OUT parameters are allowed.
- The datatypes of the function's parameters and RETURN must be compatible with RDBMS datatypes. You cannot have arguments or RETURN types like BOOLEAN, programmer-defined record, associative array, etc.
- The parameters passed to the function must use positional notation; named notation is not supported.
- The function must be stored in the database, not in a local program, Developer/2000 PL/SQL library, or form.

Calling Packaged Functions in SQL

Prior to Oracle8*i*, it was necessary to assert the purity level of a packaged procedure or function when using it directly or indirectly in a SQL statement. Beginning with Oracle8*i*, the PL/SQL runtime engine determines a program's purity level automatically if no assertion exists. The RESTRICT_REFERENCES pragma is still supported for backward compatibility, but has been deprecated in Oracle9*i*.

The RESTRICT_REFERENCES pragma asserts a purity level. The syntax for the RESTRICT_REFERENCES pragma is:

```
PRAGMA RESTRICT_REFERENCES (program_name | DEFAULT,
    purity_level);
```

The keyword DEFAULT applies to all methods of an object type or all programs in a package.

There can be from one to five purity levels, in any order, in a comma-delimited list. The purity level describes to what extent the program or method is free of *side effects*. Side effects are listed in the following table with the purity levels they address:

Purity level	Description	Restriction
WNDS	Write No Database State	Executes no INSERT, UPDATE, or DELETE statements.
RNDS	Read No Database State	Executes no SELECT statements.
WNPS	Write No Package State	Does not modify any package variables.
RNPS	Read No Package State	Does not read any package variables.
TRUST	--	Does not enforce the restrictions declared but allows the compiler to trust they are true.

Column/Function Name Precedence

If your function has the same name as a table column in your SELECT statement and the function has no parameter, then the column takes precedence over the function. To force the RDBMS to resolve the name to your function, prepend the schema name to it:

```
CREATE TABLE emp(new_sal NUMBER ...);
CREATE FUNCTION new_sal RETURN NUMBER IS ...;

SELECT new_sal FROM emp;        -- Resolves to column.
SELECT scott.new_sal FROM emp;  -- Resolves to function.
```

Oracle's Object-Oriented Features

In Oracle, an *object type* combines attributes (data structures) and methods (functions and procedures) into a single programming construct. The object type construct allows programmers to define their own reusable datatypes for use in PL/SQL programs and table and column definitions. An object type must be created in a database before it can be used in a PL/SQL program.

An instance of an object type is an *object* in the same way that a variable is an instance of a scalar type. Objects are either *persistent* (stored in the database) or *transient* (stored only in PL/SQL variables). Objects can be stored in a database as a row in a table (a row object) or as a column in a table. A table of row objects can be created with syntax such as this:

```
CREATE TABLE table_name OF object_type;
```

When stored in such a table, the object (row) has an OID (Object IDentifier) that is unique throughout the database.

Object Types

An object type has two parts: the specification and the body. The specification is required and contains the attributes and method specifications. The syntax for creating the object type specification is:

```
CREATE [OR REPLACE] TYPE obj_type_name
[AUTHID { CURRENT_USER | DEFINER } ]
{ { IS | AS } OBJECT | UNDER parent_type_name }
(
   attribute_name datatype,...,
   [ [NOT] OVERRIDING ] [ {NOT] FINAL ] [ {NOT}
   INSTANTIABLE ] method_spec,...,]
   [PRAGMA RESTRICT_REFERENCES(program_name, purities)]
)
[ [NOT] FINAL ]
[ [NOT] INSTANTIABLE ];
```

Where *method_spec* is one of the following:

```
MEMBER { PROCEDURE | FUNCTION } program_spec
```

or:

```
STATIC { PROCEDURE | FUNCTION } program_spec
```

or:

```
{ ORDER | MAP } MEMBER FUNCTION comparison_function_spec
```

or:

```
CONSTRUCTOR FUNCTION constructor_function_spec
```

Attribute specifications must appear before method specifications. Object attributes, like table columns, are defined with a name and a datatype. The name can be any legal identifier, and the datatype can be almost any datatype known to SQL other than LONG, LONG RAW, ROWID, and UROWID. Attributes can be declared on other programmer-defined object types or collection types, but not on the Oracle9*i* types ANYTYPE, ANYDATA, or ANYDATASET. Attributes cannot be of datatypes unique to PL/SQL, such as BOOLEAN.

Method headers appear in the object type specification in a comma-delimited list. Unlike in a package specification, commas (not semicolons) terminate the object type program specifications. To support object comparisons and sorting, the type can optionally include one comparison method—either ORDER or MAP. Member methods can be overloaded in object types following the same rules as function and procedure overloading in packages.

Method "specs" that appear above in the syntax can actually be call specs for Java classes in the database or for external procedures written in C.

The syntax for creating the object type body is:

```
CREATE [OR REPLACE] TYPE BODY obj_type_name
{ IS | AS }
(
   [ { ORDER | MAP } MEMBER FUNCTION
     comparison_function_body; ]
   [ { MEMBER | STATIC } { FUNCTION | PROCEDURE }
     program_body;]...
)
;
```

Again, the program bodies can be call specs to Java or C programs. The keywords CONSTRUCTOR, UNDER, FINAL, and INSTANTIABLE are all new with Oracle9*i*.

Type Inheritance (Oracle9i)

Beginning with Oracle9*i*, you can define subtypes of object types following a single-inheritance model. Oracle does not have a master root-level object type of the kind that you might find in other object programming models; instead; each type is "standalone" unless declared otherwise.

The UNDER keyword specifies that the type exists as a subtype in a hierarchy. When you are using UNDER, the parent type must be marked NOT FINAL. By default, types are FINAL, meaning that you cannot declare a subtype of that type.

A subtype contains all of the attributes and methods of its parent (supertype) and may contain additional attributes and methods. Methods can override corresponding methods from the parent. Changes to the supertype—such as the addition of attributes or methods—are automatically reflected in the subtypes.

By default, object types are INSTANTIABLE—that is, an invoking program may create an object of that type. The phrase NOT INSTANTIABLE tells Oracle that you don't want any objects of the type, in which case Oracle will not create a constructor for it. This variation generally makes sense only with types that will serve as parents of other types.

Methods

There are four kinds of methods: member, static, constructor, and comparison.

Member methods

A member method is a procedure or function designated with the keyword MEMBER. Calling programs may invoke such a method only on objects that have been instantiated.

Static methods

A static method has no access to a current (SELF) object. Such a method is declared using the keyword STATIC and can be invoked at any time using *type.method* syntax.

Constructor methods

Even if you don't declare any methods, every instantiable object has a default constructor method which allows a calling program to create new objects of that type. This built-in method:

- Has the same name as the object type
- Is a function that returns an object of that type
- Accepts attributes in named or positional notation
- Must be called with a value (or NULL) for every attribute—there is no DEFAULT clause for object attributes
- Cannot be modified

Oracle9*i* programmers can replace this default constructor with their own using the CONSTRUCTOR FUNCTION syntax. This method must have the same name as the object type, but there are no restrictions on its parameter list. The RETURN clause of the constructor's header must be RETURN SELF AS RESULT. Oracle supports the overloading of programmer-defined constructors. All non-static methods have the implied parameter SELF, which refers to the current instance of the object. The default mode for the SELF parameter is IN for functions and IN OUT for procedures. A programmer can alter the mode by explicitly including SELF in the formal parameter list.

Comparison methods

The comparison methods, ORDER and MAP, establish ordinal positions of objects for comparisons such as "<" or "between" and for sorting (ORDER BY, GROUP BY,

DISTINCT). Oracle invokes a comparison method automatically whenever it needs to perform such an operation.

MAP and ORDER methods are actually special types of member methods—that is, they only execute in the context of an existing object. An ORDER function accepts two parameters: SELF and another object of the same type. It must return an INTEGER value as explained in the following table:

Return value	Object comparison
Any negative integer (commonly -1)	SELF < second object
0	SELF = second object
Any positive integer (commonly 1)	SELF > second object
NULL	Undefined comparison: attributes needed for the comparison are NULL

For example, the Senate ranks majority party members higher than non-majority party members and within the majority (or non-majority) by years of service. Here is an example ORDER function incorporating these rules:

```
CREATE TYPE senator_t AS OBJECT (
   majority boolean_t,
   yrs_service NUMBER,
   ORDER MEMBER FUNCTION ranking (other IN
      senator_t)
      RETURN INTEGER  );

CREATE OR REPLACE TYPE BODY senator_t AS
   ORDER MEMBER FUNCTION ranking (other IN
      senator_t)
      RETURN INTEGER
   IS
   BEGIN
      IF SELF.majority.istrue()
         AND other.majority.istrue()
      THEN
         RETURN SIGN(SELF.yrs_service -
            other.yrs_service);
      ELSIF SELF.majority.istrue()
         AND other.majority.isfalse()
```

```
      THEN
         RETURN 1;
      ELSIF SELF.majority.isfalse( )
         AND other.majority.istrue( )
      THEN
         RETURN -1;
      ELSIF SELF.majority.isfalse( )
         AND other.majority.isfalse( )
      THEN
         RETURN SIGN(SELF.yrs_service -
            other.yrs_service);
      END IF;
   END ranking;
END;
```

A MAP function accepts no parameters and returns a scalar datatype such as DATE, NUMBER, or VARCHAR2 for which Oracle already knows a collating sequence. The MAP function translates, or *maps*, each object into this scalar datatype space.

If no ORDER or MAP function exists for an object type, SQL, but not PL/SQL, supports only limited equality comparisons of objects. Objects are equal if they are of the same object type and if each attribute is equal.

Use MAP if possible when frequently sorting or comparing a large number of objects, as in a SQL statement; an internal optimization reduces the number of function calls. With ORDER, the function must run once for every comparison.

Methods in Subtypes (Oracle9i)

The method modifiers OVERRIDING, FINAL, and NOT INSTANTIABLE specify how method overriding works in the subtype:

OVERRIDING
   Tells Oracle that the subtype's method will override the supertype's method.

FINAL
   Tells Oracle that new subtypes may not override this method.

NOT INSTANTIABLE
> Tells Oracle that this method is not available in the subtype.

As you can imagine, certain combinations of these modifiers are disallowed.

Oracle9*i* supports *dynamic method dispatch* to determine which overridden method to invoke at runtime. That is, it will choose the method in the most specific subtype associated with the currently instantiated object.

Manipulating Objects in PL/SQL and SQL

Variables declared as objects begin their life *atomically null*, meaning that the expression:

```
object IS NULL
```

evaluates to TRUE. Attempting to assign values to the attributes of an atomically null object will return an ACCESS_INTO_NULL exception. Instead, you must initialize the object, in one of these ways:

- Use either the default constructor method or a user-defined constructor
- Assign to it the value of an existing object
- Use SELECT INTO or FETCH INTO

Here is an example using each initialization technique:

```
DECLARE
    project_boiler_plate  project_t;
    build_web_site        project_t;

    -- Initialize via constructor.
    new_web_mgr  proj_mgr_t :=
        proj_mgr_t('Ruth', 'Home Office');

    -- Initialize via Oracle9i user-defined constructor
    -- that provides defaults
    new_web_mgr proj_mgr_t := NEW proj_mgr_t( );
```

```
      CURSOR template_cur IS
         SELECT VALUE(proj)
           FROM projects
          WHERE project_type = 'TEMPLATE'
            AND  sub_type = 'WEB SITE';
   BEGIN
      OPEN template_cur;
      -- Initialize via FETCH INTO.
      FETCH template_cur
         INTO project_boiler_plate;

      -- Initialize via assignment.
      build_web_site := project_boiler_plate;
      ...
```

After an object is initialized, it can be stored in the database, and you can then locate and use that object with the REF, VALUE, and DEREF operators.

Upcasting and Downcasting (Oracle9i)

Oracle9*i* supports implicit upcasting (widening) of a subtype and provides the TREAT operator to downcast (narrow) a supertype. TREAT can also explicitly upcast a subtype.

Assuming that book_t is a subtype of catalog_item_t, the following example shows both upcasts and downcasts:

```
DECLARE
   my_book book_t := NEW book_t();
   your_book book_t;
   some_catalog_item catalog_item_t;
BEGIN
   /* An implied upcast */
   some_catalog_item := my_book;

   /* An explicit downcast */
   your_book := TREAT(some_catalog_item AS book_t);
END;
```

The syntax of TREAT is:

```
TREAT (object_instance AS [ REF ] type)
```

where *object_instance* is a value that is of a particular supertype in an object hierarchy, and *type* is the name of subtype (or supertype) in the same hierarchy. The TREAT expression won't compile if you attempt to cast a type to another from a different type hierarchy. If you supply an object from the correct type hierarchy, TREAT will return either the casted object or NULL—but not an error.

You can also use dot notation to obtain access to the casted object's attributes and methods:

```
TREAT (object_instance AS type).{ attribute |
      method(args...) } ]
```

SQL also supports TREAT and implied upcasting.

REF operator

REF, short for REFerence, designates a datatype modifier or an operator to retrieve a logical pointer to an object. This pointer encapsulates the OID and can simplify navigation among related database objects. The syntax for a REF operator is:

```
REF(table_alias_name)
```

For example:

```
SELECT REF(p) FROM pets p WHERE ...
```

A PL/SQL variable can hold a reference to a particular object type:

```
DECLARE
   petref REF Pet_t;
BEGIN
   SELECT REF(p) INTO petref FROM pets p WHERE ...
```

Through deletions, REFs can reference a nonexistent object—called a dangling REF—resulting in a state that can be detected with the IS DANGLING predicate. For example:

```
UPDATE pets
   SET owner_ref = NULL
 WHERE owner_ref IS DANGLING.
```

Oracle's built-in package UTL_REF provides programmatic access to stored objects via their REF.

VALUE operator

Use the VALUE operator to retrieve a row object as a single object rather than multiple columns. The syntax for the VALUE operator is:

```
VALUE(table_alias_name)
```

For example:

```
SELECT VALUE(p) FROM pets p WHERE ...
```

DEREF operator

Use the DEREF operator to retrieve the value of an object for which you have a REF. The syntax for DEREF is:

```
DEREF(table_alias_name)
```

For example:

```
DECLARE
    person_ref    REF person_t;
    author        person_t;
BEGIN
    -- Get the ref.
    SELECT REF(p) INTO person_ref
       FROM persons WHERE p.last_name ='Pribyl';

    -- Dereference the pointer back to the value.
    SELECT DEREF(person_ref) INTO author FROM dual;
    ...
```

In addition, Oracle uses an OID internally as a unique key to each object. As with a ROWID, you don't typically use an OID directly.

The following table shows ways of referencing persistent objects:

Scheme	Description	Applications
OID	An opaque, globally unique handle, produced when the object is stored in the database as a table (row) object.	This is the persistent object's handle; it's what REFs point to. Your program never uses it directly.

Scheme	Description	Applications
VALUE	An operator. In SQL, it acts on an object in an object table and returns the object's *contents*. Different from the VALUES keyword found in some INSERT statements.	Allows quasi-normalizing of object-relational databases and joining of object tables using dot navigation. In PL/SQL, REFs serve as input/output variables.
REF	A pointer to an object. May be used within a SQL statement as an operator or in a declaration as a type modifier.	Used when fetching a table (row) object into a variable, or when you need to refer to an object table as an object instead of a list of columns.
DEREF	Reverse pointer lookup for REFs.	Used for retrieving the contents of an object when all you know is its REF.

Changing Object Types

You can add methods, but not attributes, to an object type stored in the database using the ALTER TYPE statement. There are several forms of this statement:

```
ALTER TYPE typename
    { ADD | MODIFY | DROP } ATTRIBUTE attribute_spec
    { INVALIDATE | CASCADE
    { [ NOT ] INCLUDING TABLE DATA | CONVERT TO SUBSTITUTABLE
}
    [ FORCE ] };

ALTER TYPE typename
    [ NOT ] { INSTANTIABLE | FINAL }
    { INVALIDATE | CASCADE
        { [ NOT ] INCLUDING TABLE DATA |
            CONVERT TO SUBSTITUTABLE }
        [ FORCE ] };

ALTER TYPE typename
    COMPILE [ DEBUG ] [ SPECIFICATION | BODY ]
            [ REUSE SETTINGS ];
```

Because altering the structure of a type can have quite a few repercussions on database objects, Oracle requires you either to INVALIDATE the dependent objects or to CASCADE the change.

When making a change from FINAL to NOT FINAL and cascading the change, you can cause existing table objects to be either NOT SUBSTITUTABLE (the default) or SUBSTITUTABLE. The following is an example of adding an attribute:

```
ALTER TYPE catalog_item_t
    ADD ATTRIBUTE publication_date VARCHAR2(400)
    CASCADE INCLUDING TABLE DATA;
```

The next example shows adding a method:

```
ALTER TYPE catalog_item_t
    ADD MEMBER PROCEDURE save,
    CASCADE;
```

After adding a method to a spec, you would use CREATE OR REPLACE TYPE BODY to implement it in the body (include all the other methods as well).

There are a variety of restrictions on modifying types; for example, you cannot change a type from INSTANTIABLE to NOT INSTANTIABLE if you have created tables that depend on the type.

The syntax for dropping an object type is:

```
DROP TYPE type_name [FORCE];
```

You can drop only an object type that has not been implemented in a table (or you can drop the tables first). The FORCE option will drop object types even if they have dependencies, but FORCE will irreversibly invalidate any dependent objects such as tables. FORCE does not do a DROP CASCADE.

If you are dropping a type whose parent type has table dependents, this form of the statement:

```
DROP TYPE subtype_name VALIDATE;
```

will "validate" the safety of dropping the subtype before performing it. That is, Oracle will only perform the drop if there are no objects of the subtype in any substitutable columns of the parent type.

Collections

There are three types of collections: associative arrays (formerly known as index-by tables or PL/SQL tables), nested tables, and VARRAYs.

Associative arrays
> Single-dimension, unbounded collections of homogeneous elements available only in PL/SQL, not in the database. Associative arrays are initially sparse; they have nonconsecutive subscripts.

Nested tables
> Single-dimension, unbounded collections of homogeneous elements available in both PL/SQL and the database as columns or tables. Nested tables are initially dense (they have consecutive subscripts), but they can become sparse through deletions.

VARRAYs
> Variable-size arrays. Single-dimension, bounded collections of homogeneous elements available in both PL/SQL and the database. VARRAYs are never sparse. Unlike nested tables, their element order is preserved when you store and retrieve them from the database.

The following table compares these similar collection types:

	Collection type		
Characteristic	Associative array	Nested table	VARRAY
Dimensionality	Single	Single	Single
Usable in SQL?	No	Yes	Yes
Usable as a column datatype in a table?	No	Yes; data stored "out of line" (in a separate table)	Yes; data typically stored "in line" (in the same table)
Uninitialized state	Empty (cannot be NULL); elements are undefined	Atomically null; illegal to reference elements	Atomically null; illegal to reference elements

	Collection type		
Initialization	Automatic, when declared	Via constructor, fetch, assignment	Via constructor, fetch, assignment
In PL/SQL, elements referenced by	BINARY_INTEGER (-2,147,483,647 .. 2,147,483,647) or character string (VARCHAR2); maximum length of VARCHAR2 is 30, minimum length is 1	Positive integer between 1 and 2,147483,647	Positive integer between 1 and 2,147483,647
Sparse?	Yes	Initially no; after deletions, yes	No
Bounded?	No	Can be extended	Yes
Can assign a value to any element at any time?	Yes	No; may need to EXTEND first	No; may need to EXTEND first, and cannot EXTEND past the upper bound
Means of extending	Assign value to element with a new subscript	Use built-in EXTEND or TRIM function to condense, with no predefined maximum	Use EXTEND or TRIM, but only up to declared maximum size.
Can be compared for equality?	No	No	No
Elements retain ordinal position and subscript when stored and retrieved from the database	N/A—can't be stored in database	No	Yes

Declaring a Collection

Collections are implemented as TYPEs. As with any programmer-defined type, you must first define the type; then you can declare instances of that type. The TYPE definition can be stored in the database or declared in the PL/SQL program. Each instance of the TYPE is a collection.

The syntax for declaring an associative array is:

```
TYPE type_name IS TABLE OF element_type [NOT NULL]
   INDEX BY {BINARY_INTEGER | VARCHAR2 (size_limit)};
```

The syntax for a nested table is:

```
[CREATE [OR REPLACE]] TYPE type_name IS TABLE OF
   element_type [NOT NULL];
```

The syntax for a VARRAY is:

```
[CREATE [OR REPLACE]] TYPE type_name IS VARRAY |
   VARYING ARRAY (max_elements) OF element_type
   [NOT NULL];
```

The CREATE keyword defines the statement to be DDL and indicates that this type will exist in the database. The optional OR REPLACE keywords are used to rebuild an existing type, preserving the privileges. *type_name* is any valid identifier that will be used later to declare the collection. *max_elements* is the maximum size of the VARRAY. *element_type* is the type of the collection's elements. All elements are of a single type, which can be most scalar datatypes, an object type, or a REF object type. If the elements are objects, the object type itself cannot have an attribute that is a collection. Explicitly disallowed collection datatypes are BOOLEAN, NCHAR, NCLOB, NVARCHAR2, REF CURSOR, TABLE, and VARRAY.

NOT NULL indicates that a collection of this type cannot have any null elements. However, the collection can be atomically null (uninitialized).

Initializing Collections

Initializing an associative array is trivial—simply declaring it also initializes it. Initializing a nested table or a VARRAY can be done in any of three ways: explicitly with a constructor, or implicitly with a fetch from the database or with a direct assignment of another collection variable.

The constructor is a built-in function with the same name as the collection. It constructs the collection from the elements passed to it. The first example shows how you can create a nested table of colors and explicitly initialize it to three elements with a constructor:

```
DECLARE
   TYPE colors_tab_t IS TABLE OF VARCHAR2(30);

   colors_tab_t('RED','GREEN','BLUE');
BEGIN
```

The next example shows how you can create the nested table of colors and implicitly initialize it with a fetch from the database:

```
-- Create the nested table to exist in the database.
CREATE TYPE colors_tab_t IS TABLE OF VARCHAR2(32);

-- Create table with nested table type as column.
CREATE TABLE color_models
(model_type   VARCHAR2(12)
,colors       color_tab_t)
NESTED TABLE colors STORE AS
   color_model_colors_tab;

-- Add some data to the table.
INSERT INTO color_models
   VALUES('RGB',color_tab_t('RED','GREEN','BLUE'));
INSERT INTO color_models
   VALUES('CYMK',color_tab_t('CYAN','YELLOW',
      'MAGENTA' 'BLACK'));

-- Initialize a collection of colors from the table.
DECLARE
   basic_colors colors_tab_t;
BEGIN
   SELECT colors INTO basic_colors
     FROM color_models
    WHERE model_type = 'RGB';
...
END;
```

The third example shows how you can implicitly initialize the table via an assignment from an existing collection:

```
DECLARE
   basic_colors Color_tab_t :=
      Color_tab_t ('RED','GREEN','BLUE');

   my_colors Color_tab_t;
BEGIN
   my_colors := basic_colors;
   my_colors(2) := 'MUSTARD';
```

Adding and Removing Elements

Elements in an associative array can be added simply by referencing new subscripts. To add elements to nested tables or VARRAYs, you must first enlarge the collection with the EXTEND function, and then you can assign a value to a new element using one of the methods described in the previous section.

Use the DELETE function to remove an element in a nested table regardless of its position. The TRIM function can also be used to remove elements, but only from the end of a collection. To avoid unexpected results, do not use both DELETE and TRIM on the same collection.

Collection Pseudo-Functions

There are several pseudo-functions defined for collections: CAST, MULTISET, and TABLE.

CAST
   Maps a collection of one type to a collection of another type.

```
SELECT column_value
FROM TABLE(SELECT CAST(colors AS color_tab_t)
            FROM color_models_a
            WHERE model_type ='RGB');
```

MULTISET

Maps a database table to a collection. With MULTISET and CAST, you can retrieve rows from a database table as a collection-typed column.

```
SELECT b.genus ,b.species,
       CAST(MULTISET(SELECT bh.country
                       FROM bird_habitats bh
                      WHERE bh.genus = b.genus
                        AND bh.species = b.species)
            AS country_tab_t)
  FROM birds b;
```

TABLE

Maps a collection to a database table (the inverse of MULTISET).

```
SELECT *
  FROM color_models c
 WHERE 'RED' IN (SELECT * FROM TABLE(c.colors));
```

You can use TABLE( ) to unnest a transient collection:

```
DECLARE
   birthdays Birthdate_t :=
       Birthdate_t('24-SEP-1984', '19-JUN-1993');
BEGIN
   FOR the_rec IN
      (SELECT COLUMN_VALUE
         FROM TABLE(CAST(birthdays AS Birthdate_t)))
```

Collection Methods

There are a number of built-in functions (methods) defined for all collections. These methods are called with dot notation:

collection_name.method_name[(parameters)]

The methods are listed in the following table:

Collection method	Description
COUNT function	Returns the current number of elements in the collection.
DELETE [(*i* [,*j*])] procedure	Removes element *i* or elements *i* through *j* from a nested table or associative array. When called with no parameters, removes all elements in the collection. Reduces the COUNT if the element is not already DELETEd. Does not apply to VARRAYs.

Collection method	Description
EXISTS (*i*) function	Returns TRUE or FALSE to indicate whether element *i* exists. If the collection is an uninitialized nested table or VARRAY, returns FALSE.
EXTEND [(*n* [,*i*])] procedure	Appends *n* elements to a collection, initializing them to the value of element *i*. *n* is optional and defaults to 1.
FIRST function	Returns the lowest index in use. Returns NULL when applied to empty initialized collections.
LAST function	Returns the greatest index in use. Returns NULL when applied to empty initialized collections.
LIMIT function	Returns the maximum number of allowed elements in a VARRAY. Returns NULL for associative arrays and nested tables.
PRIOR (*i*) function	Returns the index immediately before element *i*. Returns NULL if *i* is less than or equal to FIRST.
NEXT (*i*) function	Returns the index immediately after element *i*. Returns NULL if *i* is greater than or equal to COUNT.
TRIM [(*n*)] procedure	Removes *n* elements at the end of the collection with the largest index. *n* is optional and defaults to 1. If *n* is NULL, TRIM does nothing. Associative arrays cannot be TRIMmed.

The EXISTS function returns a BOOLEAN, and all other functions and procedures return BINARY_INTEGER except for collections indexed by VARCHAR2, which can return character strings. All parameters are of the BINARY_INTEGER type. Only EXISTS can be used on uninitialized nested tables or VARRAYs. Other methods applied to these atomically null collections will raise the COLLECTION_IS_NULL exception.

DELETE and TRIM both remove elements from a nested table, but TRIM also removes the placeholder, while DELETE does not. This behavior may be confusing, because TRIM can remove previously DELETEd elements.

Here is an example of some collection methods in use with an associative array:

```
DECLARE
   TYPE population_type IS
      TABLE OF NUMBER INDEX BY VARCHAR2(64);
```

```
      continent_population population_type;
      howmany NUMBER;
      limit VARCHAR2(64);
   BEGIN
      continent_population('Australia') := 30000000;
      -- Create new entry
      continent_population('Antarctica') := 1000;
      -- Replace old value
      continent_population('Antarctica') := 1001;
      limit := continent_population.FIRST;
      DBMS_OUTPUT.PUT_LINE (limit);
      DBMS_OUTPUT.PUT_LINE (continent_population(limit));
      limit := continent_population.LAST;
      DBMS_OUTPUT.PUT_LINE (limit);
      DBMS_OUTPUT.PUT_LINE (continent_population(limit));
   END;
   /
```

This example produces the following output:

```
Antarctica
1001
Australia
30000000
```

Here is an example of some collection methods in use with a nested table:

```
DECLARE
   TYPE colors_tab_t IS TABLE OF VARCHAR2(30);
   my_list colors_tab_t :=
      colors_tab_t('RED','GREEN','BLUE');
   element BINARY_INTEGER;
BEGIN
   DBMS_OUTPUT.PUT_LINE('my_list has '
      ||my_list.COUNT||' elements');
   my_list.DELETE(2); -- delete element two
   DBMS_OUTPUT.PUT_LINE('my_list has '
      ||my_list.COUNT||' elements');

   FOR element IN my_list.FIRST..my_list.LAST
   LOOP
      IF my_list.EXISTS(element)
      THEN
         DBMS_OUTPUT.PUT_LINE(my_list(element)
            || ' Prior= '||my_list.PRIOR(element)
            || ' Next= ' ||my_list.NEXT(element));
```

```
      ELSE
         DBMS_OUTPUT.PUT_LINE('Element '|| element
            ||' deleted. Prior= '||my_
               list.PRIOR(element)
            || ' Next= '||my_list.NEXT(element));
      END IF;
   END LOOP;
END;
```

This example produces the output:

```
my_list has 3 elements
my_list has 2 elements
RED Prior=  Next= 3
Element 2 deleted. Prior= 1 Next= 3
BLUE Prior= 1 Next=
```

Collections and Privileges

As with other TYPEs in the database, you need the EXECUTE privilege on that TYPE in order to use a collection type created by another schema (user account) in the database.

Note that Oracle9*i* Release 2 made it possible to use synonyms for user-defined TYPE names.

Nested Collections (Oracle9i)

Nested collections are collections contained in members that are collections themselves. Nesting collections is a powerful way to implement object-oriented programming constructs within PL/SQL programs. For example:

```
CREATE TYPE books IS TABLE OF VARCHAR2(64);
CREATE TYPE our_books IS TABLE OF books;
```

Bulk Binds

You can use collections to improve the performance of SQL operations executed iteratively by using *bulk binds*. Bulk binds reduce the number of context switches between the PL/SQL engine and the database engine. Two PL/SQL language constructs implement bulk binds: FORALL and BULK COLLECT INTO.

The syntax for the FORALL statement is:

```
FORALL bulk_index IN lower_bound..upper_bound
   [SAVE EXCEPTIONS]
   sql_statement;
```

bulk_index can be used only in the *sql_statement* and only as a collection index (subscript). When PL/SQL processes this statement, the whole collection, instead of each individual collection element, is sent to the database server for processing. To delete all the accounts in the collection inactives from the table ledger, do this:

```
FORALL i IN inactives.FIRST..inactives.LAST
   DELETE FROM ledger WHERE acct_no = inactives(i);
```

The default is for Oracle to stop after the first exception encountered. Use the keywords SAVE EXCEPTIONS to tell Oracle that processing should continue after encountering exceptions. The cursor attribute %BULK_EXCEPTIONS stores a collection of records containing the errors. These records have two fields, EXCEPTION_INDEX and EXCEPTION_CODE, which contain the FOR ALL iteration during which the exception was raised, as well as the SQLCODE for the exception. If no exceptions are raised, the SQL%BULK_EXCEPTION.COUNT method returns 0. For example:

```
DECLARE
   TYPE NameList IS TABLE OF VARCHAR2(32);
   name_tab NameList := NameList('Pribyl'
          ,'Dawes','Feuerstein','Gennick'
          ,'Pribyl','Beresniewicz','Dawes','Dye');
   error_count NUMBER;
   bulk_errors EXCEPTION;
   PRAGMA exception_init(bulk_errors, -24381);
BEGIN
   FORALL indx IN name_tab.FIRST..name_tab.LAST SAVE EXCEPTIONS
      INSERT INTO authors (name) VALUES (name_tab(indx));
      -- authors has pk index on name
```

```
   EXCEPTION
     WHEN others THEN
        error_count := SQL%BULK_EXCEPTIONS.COUNT;
        DBMS_OUTPUT.PUT_LINE('Number of errors is ' ||
              error_count);
        FOR indx IN 1..error_count LOOP
          DBMS_OUTPUT.PUT_LINE('Error ' || indx || '
              occurred during '||'iteration ' ||
              SQL%BULK_EXCEPTIONS(indx).ERROR_INDEX);
          DBMS_OUTPUT.PUT_LINE('Error is ' ||
            SQLERRM(-SQL%BULK_EXCEPTIONS(indx).ERROR_CODE));
        END LOOP;
END;
/

Number of errors is 2
Error 1 occurred during iteration 5
Error is ORA-00001: unique constraint (.) violated
Error 2 occurred during iteration 7
Error is ORA-00001: unique constraint (.) violated
```

The syntax for the BULK COLLECT INTO clause is:

```
BULK COLLECT INTO collection_name_list;
```

where *collection_name_list* is a comma-delimited list of collections, one for each column in the SELECT. Collections of records cannot be a target of a BULK COLLECT INTO clause. However, Oracle does support retrieving a set of typed objects and "bulk collecting" them into a collection of objects.

The BULK COLLECT INTO clause can be used in SELECT INTO, FETCH INTO, or RETURNING INTO statements. For example:

```
DECLARE
   TYPE vendor_name_tab IS TABLE OF
      vendors.name%TYPE;
   TYPE vendor_term_tab IS TABLE OF
      vendors.terms%TYPE;
   v_names vendor_name_tab;
   v_terms vendor_term_tab;
BEGIN
   SELECT name, terms
     BULK COLLECT INTO v_names, v_terms
```

```
    FROM vendors
    WHERE terms < 30;
   ...
END;
```

The next function deletes products in an input list of categories, and the SQL RETURNING clause returns a list of deleted products:

```
FUNCTION cascade_category_delete (categorylist clist_t)
RETURN prodlist_t
IS
   prodlist prodlist_t;
BEGIN
   FORALL aprod IN categorylist.FIRST..categorylist.LAST
      DELETE FROM product WHERE product_id IN
         categorylist(aprod)
         RETURNING product_id BULK COLLECT INTO prodlist;
   RETURN prodlist;
END;
```

You can use the SQL%BULK_ROWCOUNT cursor attribute for bulk bind operations. It is like an associative array containing the number of rows affected by the executions of the bulk bound statements. The *n*th element of SQL%BULK_ROWCOUNT contains the number of rows affected by the *n*th execution of the SQL statement. For example:

```
FORALL i IN inactives.FIRST..inactives.LAST
   DELETE FROM ledger WHERE acct_no = inactives(i);
FOR counter IN inactives.FIRST..inactives.LAST
LOOP
   IF SQL%BULK_ROWCOUNT(counter) = 0
   THEN
      DBMS_OUTPUT.PUT_LINE('No rows deleted for '||
         counter);
   END IF;
END LOOP;
```

You cannot pass SQL%BULK_ROWCOUNT as a parameter to another program, or use an aggregate assignment to another collection. %ROWCOUNT contains a summation of all %BULK_ROWCOUNT elements. %FOUND and

Collections | 101

%NOTFOUND reflect only the last execution of the SQL statement.

External Procedures

External procedures provide a mechanism for calling out to a non-database program, such as a DLL under NT or a shared library under Unix. Every session calling an external procedure will have its own *extproc* process started by the listener. This *extproc* process is started with the first call to the external procedure and terminates when the session exits. The shared library needs to have a corresponding library created for it in the database.

Creating an External Procedure

The following are the steps you need to follow in order to create an external procedure.

Set up the listener

External procedures require a listener. If you are running an Oracle Net database listener, it can be used as the *extproc* listener as well, although you may increase security by separating it from the external procedure listener and launching it from a privilege-limited account. Here is one way to structure the *listener.ora* file:

```
LISTENER =
   (ADDRESS = (PROTOCOL=TCP)(HOST=hostname)(PORT=1521))

EXTPROC_LISTENER =
   (ADDRESS = (PROTOCOL = IPC)(KEY = extprocKey))

SID_LIST_LISTENER =
   (SID_DESC =
      (GLOBAL_DBNAME = global_name)
      (ORACLE_HOME = oracle_home_directory)
      (SID_NAME = SID)
   )
```

```
SID_LIST_EXTPROC_LISTENER =
  (SID_DESC =
    (SID_NAME = extprocSID)
    (ORACLE_HOME = oracle_home_directory)
    (ENVS = "EXTPROC_DLLS=
      qualifier:shared_object_file_list")
    (PROGRAM = extproc)
  )
```

extprocKey

Short identifier used by Oracle Net to distinguish this listener from other potential IPC listeners. Its actual name is arbitrary, because your programs will never see it. Oracle uses EXTPROC0 as the default name for the first Oracle Net installation on a given machine. This identifier must be the same in the address list of the *listener.ora* and *tnsnames.ora* files.

extprocSID

Arbitrary unique identifier for the external procedure listener. In the default installation, Oracle uses the value PLSExtProc.

ENVS

Means of passing environment variables to the external procedure listener. The example above shows only one name/value pair, but any number of pairs are permitted. Use *name=value* syntax, separating each name/value pair with a comma, as in

```
(ENVS="LD_LIBRARY_PATH=
    /lib:/oracle/product/9.2/lib,EXTPROC_DLLS=ANY")
```

EXTPROC_DLLS

Environment variable designating non-default locations of shared libraries/DLLs. Without this setting, the default security settings of Oracle9*i* Release 2 require the library/DLL to be in the *bin* subdirectory on Windows platforms, and in Oracle's *lib* subdirectory on Unix. The *qualifier* is actually optional; if it is not present, the additional files given in a colon-delimited *shared_object_file_list* are allowed. If *qualifier* is present, it must be one of the keywords ALL (no location checking) or ONLY (disallows the default locations).

Here is an example ENVS entry supporting two shared libraries found in non-default locations:

```
(ENVS="EXTPROC_DLLS=ONLY:/u01/app/oracle/admin/local/lib/
    extprocsh.so:/u01/app/oracle/admin/local/lib/
    RawdataToPrinter.so")
```

Installations unconcerned with security may wish to permit any location using an entry such as the following:

```
(ENVS="EXTPROC_DLLS=ALL")
```

See the *Oracle9i Application Developers Guide - Fundamentals* or the *Oracle9i Net Services Administrators Guide* for more details on configuring external procedures and your listener.

Identify or create the shared library or DLL

This step has nothing to do with PL/SQL and may or may not have anything to do with the database. You must write your own C routines and link them into a shared library/DLL or use an existing library's functions or procedures. In the simple example in the next section, we will use the existing random-number–generating calls available from the operating system.

Create the library in the database

Create a library in the database for the shared library or DLL using the CREATE LIBRARY statement:

```
CREATE [OR REPLACE] LIBRARY library_name
{ IS | AS }
  'absolute_path_and_file'
  [ AGENT 'agent_db_link'];
```

The optional AGENT clause represents a database link associated with the service name of an external procedure listener. In this way the library can invoke a separate runtime instantiation of the *extproc* process. This process can run on a different database server, although that server must still reside on the same machine as the calling program.

To remove libraries from the database, you use the DROP LIBRARY statement:

```
DROP LIBRARY library_name;
```

To call out to the C runtime library's *rand* function, you don't have to code any C routines at all, because the call is already linked into a shared library, and because its arguments are directly type-mappable to PL/SQL. If the *rand* function is in the standard */lib/libc.so* shared library, as on Solaris, you would issue the following CREATE LIBRARY statement:

```
CREATE OR REPLACE LIBRARY libc_l AS
    '/lib/libc.so'; -- References C runtime library.
```

This is the typical corresponding statement for Microsoft Windows:

```
CREATE OR REPLACE LIBRARY libc_l AS
    'C:\WINDOWS\SYSTEM32\CRTDLL.DLL';
```

Create the PL/SQL wrapper for the external procedure

The syntax for the wrapper procedure is:

```
CREATE [OR REPLACE] PROCEDURE proc_name
    [parm_list]
{ AS | IS } LANGUAGE C
    [NAME external_name]    LIBRARY library_name
    [ AGENT IN (formal_parameter_name) ]
    [WITH CONTEXT]
    [PARAMETERS (external_parameter_list)];
```

where:

proc_name
  Name of the wrapper procedure.

library_name
  Name of the library created with the CREATE LIBRARY statement.

agent_name
> This clause is a way of designating a different agent process, similar to the AGENT clause on the library, but deferring the selection of the agent until runtime. You will pass in the value of the agent as a formal PL/SQL parameter to the call spec; it will supersede the name of the agent given in the library, if any.

external_name
> Name of the external routine as it appears in the library. It defaults to the wrapper package name. PL/SQL package names are usually saved in uppercase, so the *external_name* may need to be enclosed in double quotes to preserve case.

WITH CONTEXT
> Used to pass a context pointer to the external routine, so it can make Oracle Call Interface (OCI) calls back to the database.

PARAMETERS
> Identify the *external_parameter_list*, which is a comma-delimited list containing the position and datatype of parameters that get passed to the external routine. For more details on the *external_parameter_list*, see the next section, "Parameters."

The wrapper PL/SQL function or procedure is often in a package. Using the preceding random number generator example, we could create the wrapper package as follows:

```
CREATE OR REPLACE PACKAGE random_utl
AS
    FUNCTION rand RETURN PLS_INTEGER;
    PRAGMA RESTRICT_REFERENCES(rand,WNDS,RNDS,WNPS,RNPS);

    PROCEDURE srand (seed IN PLS_INTEGER);
    PRAGMA RESTRICT_REFERENCES(srand,WNDS,RNDS,WNPS,RNPS);
END random_utl;

CREATE PACKAGE BODY random_utl
AS
```

```
    FUNCTION rand RETURN PLS_INTEGER
    IS
        LANGUAGE C       -- Language of routine.
        NAME "rand"      -- Function name in the
        LIBRARY libc_l;  -- The library created above.

    PROCEDURE srand (seed IN PLS_INTEGER)
    IS
        LANGUAGE C
        NAME "srand"     -- Name is lowercase in this
        LIBRARY libc_l
        PARAMETERS (seed ub4); --Map to unsigned INT
END random_utl;
```

To use this external random number function, we simply call the package procedure srand to seed the generator, then the package function rand to get random numbers:

```
DECLARE
    random_nbr  PLS_INTEGER;
    seed        PLS_INTEGER;
BEGIN
    SELECT TO_CHAR(SYSDATE,'SSSSS') INTO seed
        FROM dual;

    random_utl.srand(seed);   -- Seed the generator.

    random_nbr := random_utl.rand; -- Get the number.
    DBMS_OUTPUT.PUT_LINE('number='||random_nbr);

    random_nbr := random_utl.rand; -- Get the number.
    DBMS_OUTPUT.PUT_LINE('number='||random_nbr);
END;
```

You can generate random numbers without the complexity or overhead of an external call by using the built-in package DBMS_RANDOM. To learn more about DBMS_RANDOM and other built-ins, check out *Oracle Built-in Packages*.

Parameters

When it comes to passing PL/SQL variables to C variables, we encounter many inconsistencies. For example, PL/SQL supports nullity, while C does not; PL/SQL can have variables in different character sets, while C cannot; and the datatypes in PL/SQL do not directly map to C datatypes.

The PARAMETERS clause specifies the external parameter list, a comma-delimited list containing parameters. The syntax for these parameters (other than CONTEXT) is:

```
{ pname | RETURN | SELF } [ property ] [ BY REFERENCE ]
   [ external_datatype ]
```

If your call spec includes WITH CONTEXT, the corresponding element in the parameter list is simply:

```
CONTEXT
```

The keyword CONTEXT indicates the position in the parameter list at which the context pointer will be passed. By convention, CONTEXT appears as the first parameter in the external parameter list.

The keyword RETURN indicates that the descriptions are for the return value from the external routine. By default, RETURN is passed by value. You can use the keywords BY REFERENCE to pass by reference (use pointers).

parameter_name is a PL/SQL formal parameter name. By default, IN formal parameters are passed by value. You can use the keywords BY REFERENCE to pass by reference (as a pointer). IN OUT and OUT formal parameters are always passed by reference.

property breaks out further to the general syntax:

```
INDICATOR | INDICATOR STRUCT | LENGTH | MAXLEN | TDO |
CHARSETID | CHARSETFORM
```

INDICATOR indicates whether the corresponding parameter is NULL. In the C program, if the indicator equals the constant OCI_IND_NULL, the parameter is NULL. If the indicator equals the constant OCI_IND_NOTNULL, the indicator is not NULL. For IN parameters, INDICATOR is passed by value (by default). For IN OUT, OUT, and RETURN parameters, INDICATOR is passed by reference.

You can pass a user-defined type to an external procedure. To do so, you will typically pass three parameters: the actual object value; a TDO (Type Descriptor Object) parameter as defined in C by the Oracle Type Translator; and an INDICATOR STRUCT parameter, to designate whether the object is NULL.

LENGTH and MAXLEN can be used to pass the current and maximum length of strings or RAWs. For IN parameters, LENGTH is passed by value (by default). For IN OUT, OUT, and RETURN parameters, LENGTH is passed by reference. MAXLEN is not valid for IN parameters. For IN OUT, OUT, and RETURN parameters, MAXLEN is passed by reference and is read-only.

CHARSETID and CHARSETFORM are used to support NLS character sets. They are the same as the OCI attributes OCI_ATTR_CHARSET_ID and OCI_ATTR_CHARSET_FORM. For IN parameters, CHARSETID and CHARSETFORM are passed by value (by default) and are read-only. For IN OUT, OUT, and RETURN parameters, CHARSETID and CHARSETFORM are passed by reference and are read-only.

SELF is used if an object member function is implemented as a callout instead of a PL/SQL routine.

When moving data between PL/SQL and C, each PL/SQL datatype maps to an "external datatype," identified by a PL/SQL keyword, which in turn maps to an allowed set of C types:

PL/SQL types ↔ External datatypes ↔ C types

PL/SQL includes a special set of keywords to use as the external datatype in the PARAMETERS clause. In some cases, the external datatypes have the same name as the C types. If you pass a PL/SQL variable of type PLS_INTEGER, the corresponding default external type is INT, which maps to an int in C. But Oracle's VARCHAR2 uses the STRING external datatype, which normally maps to a char * in C.

The following table lists all of the possible datatype conversions supported by Oracle's PL/SQL-to-C interface. Note that the allowable conversions depend on both the datatype and the mode of the PL/SQL formal parameter. Default mappings are shown in bold (if ambiguous).

Datatype of PL/SQL parameter	PL/SQL keyword identifying external type	C datatypes corresponding to PL/SQL parameters that are... IN or function return values	IN OUT, OUT, or any parameter designated as being passed BY REFERENCE
Long integer family: BINARY_INTEGER, BOOLEAN, PLS_INTEGER	**INT**, UNSIGNED INT, CHAR, UNSIGNED CHAR, SHORT, UNSIGNED SHORT, LONG, UNSIGNED LONG, SB1, UB1, SB2, UB2, SB4, UB4, SIZE_T	**int**, unsigned int, char, unsigned char, short, unsigned short, long, unsigned long, sb1, ub1, sb2, ub2, sb4, ub4, size_t	Same list of types as at left, but use a pointer (e.g., the default is int * rather than int)
Short integer family: NATURAL, NATURALN, POSITIVE, POSITIVEN, SIGNTYPE	Same as above, except default is UNSIGNED INT	Same as above, except default is unsigned int	Same as above, except default is unsigned int *
Character family: VARCHAR2, CHAR, NCHAR, LONG, NVARCHAR2, VARCHAR, CHARACTER, ROWID	**STRING**, OCISTRING	**char ***, OCIString *	**char ***, OCIString *
NUMBER	OCINUMBER	OCINumber *	OCINumber *
DOUBLE PRECISION	DOUBLE	double	double *
FLOAT, REAL	FLOAT	float	float *
RAW, LONG RAW	**RAW**, OCIRAW	**unsigned char ***, OCIRaw *	**unsigned char ***, OCIRaw *
DATE	OCIDATE	OCIDate *	OCIDate *

Datatype of PL/SQL parameter	PL/SQL keyword identifying external type	C datatypes corresponding to PL/SQL parameters that are... IN or function return values	IN OUT, OUT, or any parameter designated as being passed BY REFERENCE
Timestamp family: TIMESTAMP, TIMESTAMP WITH TIME ZONE, TIMESTAMP WITH LOCAL TIME ZONE	OCIDATETIME	OCIDateTime *	OCIDateTime *
INTERVAL DAY TO SECOND, INTERVAL YEAR TO MONTH	OCIINTERVAL	OCIInterval *	OCIInterval *
BFILE, BLOB, CLOB	OCILOBLOCATOR	OCILOBLOCATOR *	OCILOBLOCATOR * *
Descriptor of user-defined type (collection or object)	TDO	OCIType *	OCIType *
Value of user-defined collection	OCICOLL	OCIColl **, OCIArray **, OCITable **	OCIColl **, OCIArray **, OCITable **
Value of user-defined object	DVOID	dvoid *	dvoid * for final types; dvoid ** for non-final types

Java Language Integration

Java™ programmers can write server-side classes that invoke SQL and PL/SQL using standard JDBC™ or SQLJ calls. PL/SQL programmers can call server-side Java methods by writing a PL/SQL cover or *call spec* for Java using Oracle DDL.

Server-side Java in Oracle may be faster than PL/SQL for compute-intensive programs, but not as nimble for database access. PL/SQL is much more efficient for database-intensive routines because, unlike Java, it doesn't have to pay the overhead for converting SQL datatypes for use inside the stored program. Oracle programmers will want to continue to use PL/SQL for programs that perform a lot of database I/O, and use Java for the best raw computation performance.

The first step in creating a *Java stored procedure* (JSP) is writing or otherwise obtaining functional Java code. Having source code is not necessary, though, so you can use class libraries from third parties. The classes must, however, meet the following requirements:

- Methods published to SQL and PL/SQL must be declared static. PL/SQL has no mechanism for instantiating non-static Java classes.
- The classes must not issue any GUI calls (for example, to AWT) at runtime.

If you write your own JSP, and it needs to connect to the database for access to tables or stored procedures, use standard JDBC and/or SQLJ calls in your code. Many JDBC and SQLJ reference materials are available to provide assistance in calling SQL or PL/SQL from Java, but be sure to review the Oracle-specific documentation that ships with your release.

Once you have the Java class in hand, either in source or *.class* file format, the next step is loading it into the database. Oracle's *loadjava* command-line utility is a convenient way to accomplish the load. Refer to Oracle's documentation for further assistance with *loadjava*.

The third step is to create a call spec for the Java method, specifying the AS LANGUAGE JAVA clause of the CREATE command. You may create a function or procedure cover as appropriate.

Finally, you may grant EXECUTE privileges on the new JSP using GRANT EXECUTE, and PL/SQL routines can now call the JSP as if it were another PL/SQL module.

Example

Let's write a simple "Hello, World" JSP that will accept an argument:

```
package oreilly.plsquick.demos;

public class Hello {
   public static String sayIt (String toWhom) {
      return "Hello, " + toWhom + "!";
   }
}
```

Saved in a file called *Hello.java*, the source code can be loaded directly into Oracle. Doing so will automatically compile the code. Here is a simple form of the *loadjava* command:

```
loadjava -user scott/tiger -oci8 oreilly/plsquick/
   demos/Hello.java
```

The *Hello.java* file follows the Java file placement convention for packages and thus exists in a subdirectory named *oreilly/plsquick/demos*.

We can fire up our favorite SQL interpreter, connect as SCOTT/TIGER, and create the call spec for the Hello.sayIt( ) method:

```
CREATE FUNCTION hello_there (to_whom IN VARCHAR2)
   RETURN VARCHAR2
   AS LANGUAGE JAVA
   NAME 'oreilly.plsquick.demos.Hello.sayIt
     (java.lang.String) return java.lang.String';
/
```

Now we can call our function very easily:

```
BEGIN
   DBMS_OUTPUT.PUT_LINE(hello_there('world'));
END;
/
```

And we get the following as the expected output:

```
Hello, world!
```

Publishing Java to PL/SQL

To write a call spec, use the AS LANGUAGE JAVA clause in a CREATE statement. The syntax for this clause is:

```
{ IS | AS } LANGUAGE JAVA
    NAME 'method_fullname [ (type_fullname,... ]
        [ RETURN type_fullname ]'
```

method_fullname is the package-qualified name of the Java class and method. It is case-sensitive and uses dots to separate parts of the package full name. *type_fullname* is the package-qualified name of the Java datatype. Notice that a simple string, not a SQL name, follows the NAME keyword.

Type mapping follows most JDBC rules regarding the legal mapping of SQL types to Java types. Oracle extensions exist for Oracle-specific datatypes.

Most datatype mappings are relatively straightforward, but passing Oracle objects of a user-defined type is harder than one would think. Oracle provides a JPublisher tool that generates the Java required to encapsulate an Oracle object and its corresponding REF. Refer to Oracle's JPublisher documentation for guidelines on usage.

The AS LANGUAGE JAVA clause is the same regardless of whether you are using Java as a standalone JSP, the implementation of a packaged program, or the body of an object type method. For example, here is the complete syntax for creating JSPs as PL/SQL-callable functions or procedures:

```
CREATE [OR REPLACE]
{ PROCEDURE procedure_name [(param[, param]...)]
  | FUNCTION function_name [(param[, param]...)]
    RETURN sql_type
}
[AUTHID {DEFINER | CURRENT_USER}]
[PARALLEL_ENABLE]
[DETERMINISTIC]
{ IS | AS } LANGUAGE JAVA
    NAME 'method_fullname [ (type_fullname,... ]
        [ RETURN type_fullname ]'
```

When using Java as the implementation of a packaged procedure or function, Oracle allows you to place the Java call spec in either the package specification (where the call spec substitutes for the subprogram specification) or in the package body (where the call spec substitutes for the subprogram body). Similarly, when using JSPs in object type methods, the Java call spec can substitute for either the object type method specification or its body.

Note that Java functions typically map to PL/SQL functions, but Java functions declared void map to PL/SQL procedures. Also, you will quickly learn that mistakes in mapping PL/SQL parameters to Java parameters become evident only at runtime.

Data Dictionary

To learn what Java library units are available in your schema, look in the USER_OBJECTS data dictionary view where the *object_type* is like 'JAVA%'. If you see a Java class with INVALID status, it has not yet been successfully resolved. Note that the names of the Java source library units need not match the names of the classes they produce.

Reserved Words

As we mentioned earlier in this book, the PL/SQL language recognizes certain identifiers (language keywords and identifiers from the STANDARD package) as having special meaning. You must not redefine these *reserved words* as identifiers in your programs.

We compiled the following table of reserved words by taking the list Oracle publishes in the V$RESERVED_WORDS data dictionary view and trying to declare them (as variables and/or procedures). If the declarations failed, we added the words to the list. Avoid using these words in your programs.

ACCESS	ADD	ALL	ALTER
AND	ANY	AS	ASC
AT	AUDIT	BEGIN	BETWEEN
BY	CASE	CHAR	CHECK
CLOSE	CLUSTER	COLUMN	COLUMNS
COMMENT	COMMIT	COMPRESS	CONNECT
CREATE	CURRENT	CURSOR	DATE
DECIMAL	DECLARE	DEFAULT	DELETE
DESC	DISTINCT	DROP	ELSE
END	EXCLUSIVE	EXISTS	FILE
FLOAT	FOR	FROM	FUNCTION
GRANT	GROUP	HAVING	IDENTIFIED
IF	IMMEDIATE	IN	INCREMENT
INDEX	INDEXES	INITIAL	INSERT
INTEGER	INTERSECT	INTO	IS
LEVEL	LIKE	LOCK	LONG
MAXEXTENTS	MINUS	MLSLABEL	MODE
MODIFY	NOAUDIT	NOCOMPRESS	NOT
NOWAIT	NULL	NUMBER	OF
OFFLINE	ON	ONLINE	OPEN
OPTION	OR	ORDER	OVERLAPS
PACKAGE	PCTFREE	PRIOR	PRIVILEGES
PROCEDURE	PUBLIC	RAW	RENAME
RESOURCE	RETURN	REVOKE	ROLLBACK
ROW	ROWID	ROWNUM	ROWS
SAVEPOINT	SELECT	SESSION	SET
SHARE	SIZE	SMALLINT	START
SUCCESSFUL	SYNONYM	SYSDATE	TABLE
THEN	TO	TRIGGER	TYPE
UID	UNION	UNIQUE	UPDATE
USE	USER	VALIDATE	VALUES
VARCHAR	VARCHAR2	VIEW	WHEN
WHENEVER	WHERE	WITH	

Index

Symbols

-- (double hyphen), specifying single-line comments, 6
/* and */, specifying multiline comments, 6

A

AGGREGATE USING keyword, 64
ALTER TYPE statement, 88–89
anchored declarations, 19
AS LANGUAGE JAVA clause, 112–115
assigning records, 52
associative arrays, 90–91
    adding/removing elements, 94
    initializing, 92
    syntax for declaring, 92
AUTHID keyword, 63
autonomous transactions, 7, 32

B

BFILE datatype, 15
binary integer datatypes, 10
BLOB datatype, 15
block structure in PL/SQL, 8
body, package, 70–72
BOOLEAN datatype, 14
Boolean literals, 3
bulk binds and collections, 98–102

C

CASE expressions, 23
CASE statements, 22
CAST pseudo-function, 94
character datatypes, 11
character set in PL/SQL, 2
CLOB datatype, 16
collections
    adding/removing elements, 94
    bulk binds and, 98–102
    declaration syntax for, 91
    initializing, 92
    methods for, 95–98
    pseudo-functions for, 94
    types of, 90–91
comments in PL/SQL, 6
COMMIT statement, 29
conditional control statements, 20–24
CONSTANT keyword, 18
constrained declarations, 18
constrained subtypes, 20
CONSTRUCTOR keyword, 79

We'd like to hear your suggestions for improving our indexes. Send email to *index@oreilly.com*.

CONTEXT keyword, 108
control statements
  conditional, 20–24
  sequential, 24
COUNT function, 95
CREATE LIBRARY statement, 104
cursor expressions, 43
cursor variables, 41
cursors in PL/SQL, 33–44

D

data dictionary views
  USER_OBJECTS, 115
  USER_STORED_SETTINGS, 64
  V$RESERVED_WORDS, 115
  V$TIMEZONE_NAMES, 13
database events and triggers, 66, 69
database interaction, 29–33
datatype conversions, 110–111
datatypes of parameters, 56
date datatypes, 12–14
datetime interval literals (Oracle9i), 4
DBMS_RANDOM built-in package, 107
DDL events and triggers, 66, 69
decimal numeric datatypes, 10
declaring
  exceptions, 44–46
  programs, 61
  records, 50
default values for parameters, 58
DELETE procedure, 95
DELETING trigger predicate, 68
delimiters in PL/SQL, 5
DEREF operator, 87
DETERMINISTIC keyword, 63
DML events and triggers, 65, 68
downcasting subtypes, 85–88

DROP event, 66, 69
dynamic cursors, 33, 40

E

exception handling, 44–50
EXCEPTION_INIT pragma, 7
EXECUTE IMMEDIATE statement, 40
EXISTS function, 96
EXIT statements, 28
explicit cursors, 33–36
expressions, cursor, 43
EXTEND procedure, 96
external procedures
  creating, 102–107
  creating PL/SQL wrappers for, 105
  parameters and, 107–111
extproc processes, 102
EXTPROC_DLLS environment variable, 103
extprocKey identifier, 103
extprocSID identifier, 103

F

FETCH statement, 35
fields of records, 50–53
FINAL keyword, 79
  methods in subtypes, 83
FIRST function, 96
floating-point numbers, datatypes for, 10
FOR EACH ROW statement, 67
FOR loops, 26
forward declarations of programs, 61
%FOUND attribute, 36
functions in PL/SQL, 54

G

GOTO statements, 24

H

handling exceptions, 44–50

I

identifiers in PL/SQL, 3
IF-THEN-ELSE statements, 20
implicit cursors, 37–39
IN parameters, 57
initializing
 collections, 92
 objects, 84
 packages, 73
INSERTING trigger
  predicate, 68
INSTANTIABLE keyword, 79
INTERVAL keyword, 4
IS DANGLING predicate., 86
IS NULL/IS NOT NULL
  syntax, 16
%ISOPEN attribute, 36

J

Java language
  integration, 111–115
Java stored procedures
  (JSPs), 112
JPublisher tool, 114

L

language fundamentals of
  PL/SQL, 2–9
large object (LOB) datatypes, 15
LAST function, 96
libraries, creating in
  database, 104
LIMIT function, 96
listeners, setting up for external
  procedures, 102–104
literals, 3
loadjava utility, 112
LOB (large object) datatypes, 15

local programs, 59
LOCK TABLE statement, 31
LOGON/LOGOFF events, 66, 69
loops in PL/SQL, 25–28

M

methods in subtypes
  (Oracle9*i*), 83
methods, types of, 80–83
modes of parameters, 57
MULTISET pseudo-function, 95
mutual recursion, 61

N

named notation, 58
NCHAR datatype, 15
NCLOB datatype, 16
nested collections, 98
nested tables, 90–91
  initializing, 93, 94
  syntax for declaring, 92
nesting records, 53
NEXT function, 96
NLS (national character set)
  datatypes, 15
  external procedures and, 109
NOCOPY option, 57
NOT INSTANTIABLE method
  modifier, 83
NOT NULL constraint, 19
%NOTFOUND attribute, 36
NULL statements, 25
NULLs in PL/SQL, 16
numeric datatypes, 10
numeric literals, 3
NVARCHAR2 datatype, 15

O

object types, changing, 88–89
object-oriented features, 77–89

OPEN FOR statement, 40
OR REPLACE keyword, 63
Oracle object-oriented features and PL/SQL, 77–89
Oracle8i
   autonomous transactions and, 7, 32
   determining purity levels of programs, 76
   SQL%BULK_ROWCOUNT attribute and, 38
Oracle9i
   CASE expressions, 23
   CASE statements, 22
   compiling stored PL/SQL programs, 63
   datetime interval datatypes, 4, 12–14
   external procedures, 103
   methods in subtypes, 83
   natively compiling stored programs, 64
   object types, 78
   type inheritance, 80
   upcasting/downcasting subtypes, 85–88
OUT parameters, 57
overloading programs, 60
OVERRIDING method modifier, 83

P

packaged functions, calling in SQL, 76
packages in PL/SQL, 69–74
PARALLEL_ENABLED keyword, 63
parameters, 56–65
   default values for, 58
   external procedures and, 107–111
   modes of, 57

passing arguments in parameter lists, 58
PIPE ROW command, 62
PIPELINED keyword, 63
PLS_INTEGER datatype, 11
positional notation, 58
PRAGMA keyword, 7
predicates, trigger, 68
PRIOR function, 96
privileges and stored PL/SQL, 65
procedures in PL/SQL, 54
propagating exceptions, 47
purity levels of programs, determining, 76

R

raising exceptions, 46
records in PL/SQL, 50–53
recursion, mutual, 61
REF operator, 86
REF_CURSOR types, 41
referencing fields of records, 51
REPEAT UNTIL loop emulation, 28
reserved words in PL/SQL, 3, 115
RESTRICT_REFERENCES pragma, 7, 76
RETURN keyword, 108
ROLLBACK statement, 30
%ROWCOUNT attribute, 36
%ROWTYPE attribute, 19

S

SAVEPOINT statement, 30
scalar datatypes, 10–15
scope of exceptions, 47
searched CASE expressions, 23
searched CASE statements, 22
SELECT FOR UPDATE clause, 38

sequential control statements, 24
SERIALLY_REUSABLE pragma, 7, 73
SERVERERROR event, 66, 69
SET TRANSACTION statement, 30
SHUTDOWN event, 66, 69
specification, package, 70–72
SQL statements, calling stored functions from, 74–77
SQL%BULK_ROWCOUNT attribute, 38
SQL%FOUND attribute, 38
SQL%ISOPEN attribute, 37
SQL%NOTFOUND attribute, 38
SQL%ROWCOUNT attribute, 38
SQLCODE function, 49
SQLERRM function, 49
STARTUP event, 66, 69
statements in PL/SQL, 7
static cursors, 33
stored functions, calling from SQL statements, 74–77
stored programs, compiling, 63
natively, 64
string literals, 3
subtypes, constrained/unconstrained, 20

T

table functions, 62
TABLE pseudo-function, 95
time datatypes, 12–14
transaction management, 29–32
TREAT operator, 85
triggers in PL/SQL, 65–69
TRIM procedure, 96
%TYPE attribute, 19
type inheritance (Oracle9i), 80

U

unconstrained subtypes, 20
UNDER keyword, 79
upcasting subtypes, 85–88
UPDATING trigger predicate, 68
USER_OBJECTS data dictionary view, 115
USER_STORED_SETTINGS data dictionary view, 64

V

V$RESERVED_WORDS data dictionary view, 115
V$TIMEZONE_NAMES data dictionary view, 13
VALUE operator, 87
VARCHAR2 datatype, 12
variables, 9–20
  declaring, 16
  default values of, 18
VARRAYs, 90–91
  initializing, 93, 94
  syntax for declaring, 92

W

WHEN OTHERS clause, 48
WHERE CURRENT OF clause, 39
WHILE loops, 27
wrappers for external procedures, 105

Other Titles Available from O'Reilly

Oracle PL/SQL

Learning Oracle PL/SQL
Bill Pribyl & Steven Feuerstein
1st Edition November 2001
424 pages, ISBN 0-596-00180-0

Oracle PL/SQL Developer's Workbook
By Steven Feuerstein with
Andrew Odewahn
1st Edition May 2000
592 pages, ISBN 1-56592-674-9

Oracle PL/SQL Programming, 3rd Edition
By Steven Feuerstein with Bill Pribyl
3rd Edition September 2002
1018 pages, ISBN 0-596-00381-1

Oracle PL/SQL Best Practices
By Steven Feuerstein
1st Edition April 2001
202 pages, ISBN 0-596-00121-5

**Oracle Essentials:
Oracle9i, Oracle8i & Oracle8**
By Rick Greenwald, Robert Stackowiak
& Jonathan Stern
2nd Edition June 2001
381 pages, ISBN 0-596-00179-7

O'REILLY®

To order: 800-998-9938 • order@oreilly.com • www.oreilly.com
Online editions of most O'Reilly titles are available by subscription at safari.oreilly.com
Also available at most retail and online bookstores.